A Fool For Christ

The Life, Miracles, and Prophecies of Saint Gabriel of Georgia

James Mamone

A FOOL FOR CHRIST: THE LIFE, MIRACLES, AND PROPHECIES OF SAINT GABRIEL OF GEORGIA

 Formatted with Vellum

Source Acknowledgments

This biography draws extensively upon the hagiographical records, oral histories, and translations preserved by the Georgian Orthodox Church and the following publications:

• Primary Biographical Accounts: Elder's Diadem, published by the Equal-to-the-Apostles Saint Nino Convent of Samtavro (2008), translated by Ana Memarnishvili.

• Historical Narratives: The Canadian Journal of Orthodox Christianity, Volume XX, No 2 (2025); Death to the World, Issue #1 (1994); and the archives of the American Carpatho-Russian Orthodox Diocese of North America.

• Testimonies and Miracles: Accounts of healing and prophecy are derived from the recollections of Nun Paraskeva (Rostiashvili), Otar Nikolaishvili, and the sisters of Samtavro Convent, as well as articles published by OrthoChristian.com and the Catalog of Good Deeds (St. Elisabeth Convent).

Scripture Quotations

Unless otherwise indicated, all Scripture quotations are taken from the King James Version or are translations adapted from the Georgian hagiographical texts.

Disclaimer

The accounts of miracles, including the burning of the Lenin portrait, the concealment of the "foolishness", and posthumous healings, are presented as documented in the lives of the saints and witness testimonies. The medical diagnosis #666 is cited directly from the historical records of the City Psycho-Neurological Hospital, Tbilisi (1965).

Preface

In the ancient capital of Georgia, Mtskheta, within the walls of the Samtavro Convent, lies a grave that serves as a significant point of reverence for the Orthodox world. Here rests a man who was canonized a saint a mere seventeen years after his repose—an unusually short time in the history of the Church.

To the Georgian people, he is affectionately referred to as "Mama Gabrieli" (Father Gabriel), but to the broader world, he is increasingly recognized as "The Great Love of the Twentieth Century."

This book narrates the story of Archimandrite Gabriel (Urgebadze), a man whose life embodies a paradox shrouded in mystery. He was a monk who walked the streets barefoot in winter, sometimes residing in a henhouse with significant gaps in the walls, all while emanating a warmth that melted even the hardest of hearts.

He was a priest who, to the untrained eye, might have seemed like a drunkard or a madman, yet he possessed the extraordinary gift of discerning human thoughts and foreseeing the future.

To understand Saint Gabriel, one must grasp the ancient and arduous path of the *Salos*—the "Fool-for-Christ." As defined in the spiritual heritage of the East, a *Salos* adopts the guise of feeble-mindedness to conceal profound divine wisdom and sanctity.

This is an "exceptionally rare feat," particularly in contemporary times, requiring an individual to willingly relinquish their dignity to evade human acclaim. Father Gabriel donned this mask with remarkable precision. He would feign drunkenness, dance in the streets, or challenge nuns to test their humility, all while intentionally masking his sagacity. As he once confessed to a spiritual child, "When it seemed to me that I was an important person... I would act foolishly; and when people would laugh at me, I'd be humbled and see that I'm garbage."

His apparent foolishness, however, served as a weapon against a very specific evil. Father Gabriel lived and endured during the "dark years of persecution" under the Soviet communist regime, a time when churches were destroyed, clergy were executed, and innocent lives were taken.

In a world that had institutionalized atheism, Father Gabriel became a living testament to faith. He is perhaps most renowned for the day in 1965 when he set fire to a twelve-meter portrait of Lenin during a May Day demonstration, declaring to the startled crowd that glory belongs not to a corpse, but to Jesus Christ. For this act, he was brutally beaten, resulting in a fractured skull, and was subsequently diagnosed by the state as a "psychopathic personality" who believed in God and angels—a diagnosis that spared him from execution but branded him with a "White Ticket" and the medical file number 666.

Yet, *The Fool for Christ* is not merely a chronicle of suffering or eccentricity; it is a testament to the transformative power of love. Father Gabriel famously wore a placard around his neck that read, "A man without love is like a pitcher without a bottom."

He taught that in the end times, which he prophesied were imminent, humanity would be redeemed through love, humility, and kindness. His life exemplified the belief that "truth is in the immortality of the spirit," a phrase he requested be inscribed on his grave.

The following chapters draw from the memories of those who knew him—the nuns he tested, the prisoners he healed, and the spiritual children he guided. They paint a portrait of a man who was "consumed in serving others," a vessel chosen by God to navigate the trials of the twentieth century and emerge adorned with a diadem of holiness.

This work is by no means exhaustive nor, I dare say, original; as I have drawn from numerous sources, which I have listed at the end. (I aimed to avoid detracting from the enjoyment of Father Gabriel's life with excessive footnotes and citations.) It is an endeavor to deepen my understanding of my patron saint—a patron saint I did not choose, but who I feel chose me. And very aggressively, I might add. In my desire to learn more about him, I created this book, and it is my hope that others may find joy in it and discover insights they may not have previously known. There are certainly more comprehensive works available; this is more of a personal project.

As you read these pages, you are invited to look beyond the rags and the "eccentric behaviors" of the *Salos* to behold the "radiant pillar of the end times."

You are invited to meet the Saint who claimed his cross was "the whole of Georgia and half of Russia," and who promised that he would continue to assist us from beyond.

Welcome to the life of Saint Gabriel.

Chapter 1

Vasiko

"Meekness is an ever lit, God pleasing candle."

Birth and Baptism

The life of the man who would become known as the "Great Love of the Twentieth Century" began in the darkening shadow of the Soviet era. On August 26, 1929, in the Navtlughi district of Tbilisi, Georgia, a son was born to Vasili and Barbara Urgebadze.

He was baptized as an infant in the Church of the Holy Great Martyr Barbara by Tamar Begiashvili, a former "Sister of Mercy," and given the name Goderdzi.

Goderdzi was born into a world of violence and spiritual desolation; the communist regime was actively persecuting religion, destroying and closing churches, and murdering or deporting innocent people.

This atmosphere of terror touched the Urgebadze family almost immediately. When Goderdzi was approximately two years old, his father, Vasili Urgebadze—an official in the

Communist Party—was murdered under suspicious circumstances. Following this tragedy, family members began to refer to the young boy as "Vasiko" in honor of his deceased father.

Vasiko's mother, Barbara, was a woman of remarkable resilience. Beautiful in her youth, she married early at the age of fourteen and found herself a widow by twenty-two.

Left in a precarious situation with three children from her first marriage—Emma, Michael, and Goderdzi—she worked tirelessly to support her family during the severe famine of 1931, raising them with help from her stepmother. Barbara later remarried and had a daughter named Julietta.

A Unique Childhood

From his earliest years, Vasiko was an extraordinary boy, distinguished by a divine grace that set him apart from his peers.

By nature, he was a quiet child who shunned the noisy games of other children, preferring solitude. While others played, Vasiko engaged in a unique and dangerous pastime for a child living under an atheistic regime: he built small churches. Sitting quietly in the corner of his kindergarten room or in his yard, he constructed these miniature sanctuaries from pebbles and matchboxes, placing lighted matches inside them to simulate candles.

This pious activity caused his mother great distress. Barbara feared someone might witness her son's actions and report the family to the authorities.

In a time when defiance of communist ideology could lead to imprisonment or death, she worried that spies would accuse the family of raising the child in opposition to the state.

Despite the risk, the boy continued his quiet constructions.

Vasiko also exhibited an unusual affinity for the natural

world that astonished those who witnessed it. He would take a small stick in his hands and run off, with chirping birds flying down to perch on it, following him along his way.

This "bird miracle" was accompanied by a profound gentleness of spirit. Vasiko refused to permit the setting of mousetraps in his home that would kill the animals. Instead, he captured mice alive in cages and later released them outside, ensuring they were unharmed.

The Awakening

Vasiko began his formal education at the age of six.

He was a bright student for whom reading, writing, and arithmetic came easily, and he gained admiration for his kindness. However, his life changed irrevocably at seven due to a domestic quarrel he witnessed in his neighborhood.

During a confrontation between two neighbors, one exclaimed, "You have crucified me like Christ!"

The phrase struck a chord in the young boy's heart. Confused and curious, Vasiko asked the adults, "What does 'crucified' mean? And who is this Christ?" The adults, perhaps fearful or simply dismissive, directed him to the local church.

Vasiko went to the church, but like many others in Georgia at that time, it was closed or destroyed by the communists.

However, he encountered a church warden (a guard) there. Vasiko repeated his questions. The warden showed the boy an icon of the Crucifixion and advised him to read the story of Jesus Christ in the Gospel.

The Purchase of the Gospel

Driven by an earnest desire to know God, Vasiko began to save his money.

Once he gathered enough, he purchased his own copy of the Gospel. This marked the beginning of a new chapter in his life. From that day forward, he was consumed by a singular thought and devotion: to live solely for Christ.

He read the New Testament day and night, losing interest in school lessons and allocating minimal time to them in order to return to his spiritual reading.

Within a few years, he had nearly memorized the text. Before bed, he would retreat to his room, praying for extended periods in the corner before his icons.

The Vision of the Cross

As his faith deepened, Vasiko began to receive spiritual signs. He later recalled a specific incident from this period of his childhood. While sitting on the balcony of the second floor of his home, lost in thought, an inner voice commanded him to look up at the sky.

He stood up, approached the edge of the balcony, and gazed upward. There, he saw a large cross suspended in the sky.

Reflecting on this moment at the end of his life, Monk Gabriel stated, "At that time, I didn't know, but I now understand that it was the cross I had to bear out of love for God and my people."

The young boy, still known as Vasiko, had found his calling, oblivious to the heavy but glorious burden that lay ahead.

Chapter 2

The Young Confessor

The Night of the Beast

By the time Goderdzi reached the age of twelve, the grace that had settled upon him in early childhood began to manifest in both terrifying and powerful ways. He had already forsaken the games of his peers for the solitude of the Gospel, yet the spiritual realm he pursued with such fervor was poised to reveal itself not only in light but in darkness. This confrontation would ultimately seal his destiny as a warrior of Christ.

One night, while the rest of Tbilisi slept under the heavy blanket of Soviet rule, young Goderdzi lay in his bed, drifting into slumber. Suddenly, he was jolted awake. The atmosphere in the room had shifted, becoming heavy and oppressive. Before him stood a vision that would have shattered the mind of a lesser child: a demon. The entity bore a terrifying face, twisted with ancient malevolence, and horns protruded from its head. It stared at the boy with unbridled rage, a hatred so palpable it seemed to vibrate in the air.

Remarkably, the twelve-year-old did not succumb to panic. As he later recounted, "By God's mercy, I wasn't frightened, but I became tense." He did not flee, nor did he hide under his blankets. Instead, he gazed at the monstrosity in astonishment, witnessing the reality of the evil he had read about in Scripture.

Infuriated by the boy's lack of terror and his silent defiance, the demon roared, "You're fighting against me, are you?!"

In a fit of demonic fury, the entity struck the child with such supernatural force that it rendered him unconscious. When his mother, Barbara, later entered the room, she found her son lying senseless, the victim of a battle unseen by the world. God, however, had preserved the life of His chosen one.

For most, such a traumatic encounter would lead to despair or madness. For Vasiko (as his family called him), it became a foundational pillar of his theology. He did not awaken from unconsciousness with fear, but with a steely, paradoxical logic that would define his life. He later concluded, "Upon witnessing the demon, my faith in Christ grew stronger, and I declared—if the demon exists, then God exists in even greater measure."

Furthermore, the sight of the grotesque visage of the fallen angel prompted an unexpected epiphany in the boy's heart. Having witnessed the ultimate ugliness of evil, he told his friends, "I came to appreciate the beauty of human beings." In the face of absolute darkness, the young confessor saw the inherent value of the divine image of God in man.

Uncle Mukha and the Boulder

Following this initiation into spiritual warfare, the Lord began to endow Vasiko with divine power that spilled over into the physical world. The boy was no longer just a pious child; he was evolving into a vessel of grace capable of extraordinary feats that transcended natural laws.

One sweltering summer day, a neighbor named Nun Pelagia (who would later become a hegumenia) witnessed the aftermath of a miracle through her uncle's testimony. Her uncle, George, was a man of formidable physical strength. He was a wrestler known to everyone as "Uncle Mukha" (meaning "The Oak") because he was as solid and unmovable as a tree.

Uncle Mukha was walking home along the old St. Barbara road when he approached the ruins of the Church of St. George. There, under the scorching sun, he saw twelve-year-old Vasiko laboring alone. The boy was diligently clearing the devastated sanctuary of large boulders, trying to restore some dignity to the house of God. He was so absorbed in his sacred task that he did not notice the wrestler approaching.

When Vasiko finally looked up and saw the strongman, his face brightened. "Come, Uncle Mukha," he called out warmly, "and if you can, help me with this." He gestured toward a massive boulder that he needed to move.

Mukha, confident in his strength, stepped up to the stone. He grasped it firmly, braced his legs, and pulled. He exerted all his power, muscles straining, sweat streaming down his face. However, the boulder did not budge. It was rooted to the earth, too heavy even for "The Oak."

Then the small boy stepped forward. Vasiko looked at the stone that had stymied the wrestler and simply declared, "In the name of Christ!"

With those words, the twelve-year-old lifted the massive

rock and carried it over to the pile of stones he had gathered, placing it down as if it were a mere pebble. Uncle Mukha stood dumbfounded. He hurried home, proclaiming loudly to everyone he met, "Glory to Christ, our Lord! It seems He preserves His chosen ones on the earth."

The miracle had a profound effect on the wrestler. Although Mukha's family was religious, the fear of the atheist regime had distanced them from the church; they no longer fasted or attended services. However, after witnessing the power of God through the actions of a child, Uncle Mukha cast aside his fear and committed to a Christian life from that day forward.

The Boy Prophet of the War

As World War II raged, casting a shadow of grief and uncertainty over Georgia, the spiritual authority of the young Vasiko began to gain recognition within the wider community. People were desperate. Information from the frontlines was scarce, and thousands of families lived in agonizing ignorance regarding the fate of their fathers, husbands, and sons.

In their desperation, impoverished individuals began to seek out Vasiko. It was an extraordinary sight: adults approaching a twelve-year-old boy to inquire about the life and death of their relatives. They sensed that this child perceived truths hidden from the eyes of the world.

Vasiko did not turn them away. However, he refused to act as a mere soothsayer. He utilized his prophetic gift as a net to draw souls back to God. When people asked for news, he would answer them, his words consistently proving true, but he would always accompany his answer with a sermon. "Go to the church," he would preach to the grieving adults. "Don't abandon Christ and don't lose the salvation of your souls."

His clairvoyance was undeniable, and his predictions were accurate, but his objective was singular: to restore the people's trust in the Church during a time when the state was doing everything to undermine it.

The Trash Heap and the Icons

Despite the growing reverence people began to show him, Vasiko exhibited a profound humility. He intuitively understood that the praise of men can poison a monk's soul. To counter this, he engaged in behaviors that shocked his family and neighbors—early manifestations of the *Salos*, or Fool-for-Christ, he would later become.

He frequently went to the most prominent area of the neighborhood, found a pile of garbage, and sat within it. There, amidst the refuse, he would proclaim loudly for all to hear: "Always remember, Vasiko, that you are nothing but refuse, and never hold yourself in high regard."

His family was mortified. They punished him in an attempt to force him to behave like a normal child, but Vasiko remained steadfast. The neighbors, however, sensed the holiness behind the madness. They refrained from mocking him, silenced by the boy's unique dignity.

This humility was matched only by his fervor for the sacred. During the Soviet purges, fear drove many Georgians to hide their icons in attics, basements, or storage rooms. Over time, as faith waned, these sacred images were often neglected, gathering dust and disrespect.

Vasiko became a self-appointed guardian of these holy relics. He would walk through the village, approach specific houses, and knock on the doors. When the owners answered, he would speak with startling precision: "You have an icon resting in your house," he would say, indicating the exact location where it was hidden. "You should either treat it with due reverence or give it to me. I will safeguard it. If you ever wish to reclaim it, come to me, and I will gladly return it."

His knowledge of the hidden icons was inexplicable. Some people, shamed by the child's piety, repented and restored the icons to a place of honor. Others, lacking the will to care for them, surrendered the icons to the boy. Vasiko accepted them all. He cherished them with a special love, cleaning them, repairing their frames, and adorning them with materials he found. These rescued icons would eventually cover every inch of the walls and ceiling of the church he built and his cell at Samtavro, creating an atmosphere of overwhelming holiness that struck pilgrims to the core.

Margo the Fortune Teller

Following a period of wandering, during which he was rejected from monasteries due to his youth—during which he slept in the wild and visited the ascetics at Bethany and Zedazeni—Vasiko found himself back in Tbilisi. He needed a place to stay and found shelter in the unlikeliest of homes: that of a woman named Margo.

Margo was a kind-hearted woman, yet she earned her living through fortune-telling, a practice that is fundamentally at odds with Christian faith. Although Vasiko was grateful for her hospitality, he was deeply saddened that such a benevolent soul was engaged in sin and deception.

The opportunity to intervene arose when Margo fell ill. Too sick to work, she worried about her clients. Vasiko stepped forward to comfort her, making a startling promise: "I will receive the people instead of you."

When the clients arrived, expecting fortune-telling and divination, they were instead met by a pious boy with eyes that seemed to see right through them. Vasiko did not read cards or gaze into crystal balls; rather, he preached. He spoke to them about love for God and the necessity of leading a Christian life.

The visitors were astonished to find that this boy knew more about them than any fortune teller ever could. Endowed with the gift of prophecy, Vasiko began to discuss their past sins —sins they had long forgotten or concealed. He warned them of future dangers, not to dazzle them but to save them. He urged them to seek a priest for confession and to partake of Holy Communion.

The impact was electric. The clients departed not with vague predictions but with a call to repentance. Margo herself, witnessing the grace flowing through the boy and the significant impact he had on her visitors, was moved to the core. She renounced her fortune-telling, abandoned her trade, and embraced a Christian way of life. The conversion of the well-known fortune teller by the boy-preacher caused a sensation, stirring rumors and wonder throughout Tbilisi.

The Sack of Bones

As Vasiko entered his teenage years, his patriotism and love for his people deepened alongside his faith. This love was put to the test when the communist government decided to "renovate" a public park near the old Vera cemetery.

This was no ordinary cemetery; it served as the final resting place for the Georgian cadets—young soldiers who lost their lives fighting for Georgia's independence against the Soviet invasion in 1921. To the Soviet authorities, these graves represented an inconvenience, obstacles to their urban development plans. With callous disregard for both the deceased and the nation's history, they brought in bulldozers to level the ground.

The area was uprooted. The earth was churned, and the

remains of these young heroes were brought to the surface, scattered and exposed in the soil. It was a barbaric act of desecration.

Vasiko was heartbroken. He could not bear to see the remains of those who died for his country treated as refuse. In an act of quiet yet dangerous heroism, the teenager began to visit the site at night. Under the cover of darkness, risking arrest by the authorities who monitored the site, Vasiko collected the scattered bones. He gathered them reverently into sacks and carried them away, secretly reburying them in a secure location where they would not be disturbed again.

It was a grim task for a young boy to collect skulls and ribs in the night, but it demonstrated the depth of his character. He became a guardian not only of abandoned icons and lost souls but also of the very dignity of his nation.

Chapter 3

The Monk's Path

"Will everyone be saved? No. God is merciful but not to all; nobody can help you unless you strive for your salvation. Whoever saves his soul and helps his neighbor by word or deed obeys the commandments of God. Having free will, you must strive for salvation."

The Gospel in the Mire

By the time Vasiko reached his twelfth year, the spiritual chasm between him and his mother, Barbara, had widened into a divide that could no longer be bridged by silence. Barbara was a woman shaped by adversity; widowed at twenty-two, she had navigated the challenges of raising her three children—Emma, Michael, and Goderdzi— through the famine of 1931 and the terrors of the Stalinist purges with nothing but her resilience and hard work. For her, survival meant blending in, keeping one's head down, and exerting relentless effort. Her son's behavior—his refusal to engage in play, his fervent devotion to the church, and his collection of rocks and icons—was not merely eccentric; in the context of the Soviet Union, it was perilous.

She watched with increasing anxiety as her son's faith calcified into something unyielding. She pleaded with him, her voice trembling with the fear of a mother who sees her child walking toward danger. "Do not torment yourself! Live as ordinary people do!" she would beg. "Be religious, but do not let your desires be solely fixed on the Gospel and religion!" She wanted him to be safe. She wanted him to be conventional.

But Vasiko was not destined for the "ordinary." The breaking point came on a day that would irrevocably sever his childhood from his destiny. In a fit of desperate anger, driven by the fear that her son was jeopardizing his future, Barbara seized his most cherished possession—his Gospel. With a shout of frustration, she threw the Holy Book into the toilet.

For Vasiko, this was not merely an act of disrespect; it was an existential crisis. He did not scream or resist. Instead, he reached into the mire, retrieved the soiled book, and pressed it against his chest, weeping softly. The desecration of the Word of God was a sign he could not ignore. He realized he could no longer live under a roof where God was regarded as a burden.

That night, as the clock struck twelve, the twelve-year-old boy made the first significant renunciation of his life. Clutching his salvaged Gospel, he stepped out of his mother's house into the darkness. It was late autumn, and the air was biting cold. He did not look back. He walked through the night, his small figure consumed by the shadows of Tbilisi, making his way toward the ancient capital of Mtskheta.

The Wanderer

Vasiko's journey was a pilgrimage marked by rejection. He arrived in Mtskheta, the spiritual heart of Georgia, in search of a place where he could fully belong to God. His first destination was the Samtavro Convent, where the abbess, Hegumenia Anusia (Kochlamazashvili), received the shivering boy with maternal warmth. She provided him with nourishment and warmth by the fire; however, the convent's strict regulations prohibited men, let alone runaway boys, from residing within the nunnery.

With a heavy heart, she directed him to the nearby Svetitskhoveli Cathedral, home to the Living Pillar and the resting place of Christ's Robe. Vasiko approached the cathedral and prostrated himself before the Iveron Icon of the Mother of God, begging her for a cell and the privilege of living within the monastery walls. The monks sheltered him for three days. Unfortunately, the reach of the Soviet state extended even into this sanctuary; a governmental decree strictly forbade the lodging of minors in monasteries for extended periods. To shield the monastery from potential repercussions, he was compelled to leave.

Continuing his journey, he ascended the rugged path to the Shio-Mgvime Monastery, nestled in a limestone canyon. Here, too, he was given shelter for another three days before being asked to depart. He then trekked to the Zedazeni Monastery, situated high on a mountain ridge. The elderly monks, moved by the fervent zeal in the boy's eyes, developed a deep affection for him. Unable to legally house him, they devised a secret hiding place near the monastery walls—a cave-like shelter where he resided for several weeks.

But the vigilance of Soviet law enforcement was unwavering. Concerned for the boy's safety amid intensified police scrutiny, the monks were reluctantly compelled to send him away. They provided him with detailed directions and provisions for his journey, directing him toward the hidden Monastery of Bethany.

It was at Bethany that Vasiko ultimately found the spiritual fathers who would profoundly shape his soul. The monastery was home to two revered ascetics, Father George (Mkheidze) and Father John (Maisuradze). These men, who would later be canonized as saints, recognized the grace within the boy from the outset. They became his most esteemed confessors and mentors. Although he could not remain permanently, Bethany served as his spiritual anchor. Even after his mother eventually located him and begged him to return home—promising, "Please come back home and live as you wish. I won't hinder your chosen path"—Vasiko continued to journey to Bethany at least once a month to labor alongside the holy elders.

At the age of sixteen, he undertook a pilgrimage on foot to the Martkopi Monastery. There, he encountered another spiritual giant, Fr. Aitala. This meeting left a lasting impression on the young ascetic. In later years, Father Gabriel would speak of him with profound respect, recalling him as "a great monk gifted with clairvoyance." These encounters were the fires in which Vasiko's own resilience was forged, preparing him for the heavy cross of leadership and suffering that lay ahead.

The Soldier with a Secret

In 1949, the Soviet state intervened in Vasiko's life. He was conscripted into the Red Army and assigned to the border guard unit in Batumi. The military functioned as an atheistic machine, designed to grind down individuality and faith, where the collective overshadowed the soul. This seemed an unlikely environment for a mystic like Vasiko. It should have spelled spiritual demise. Instead, he did not waver and transformed his barracks into a sanctuary.

While his fellow soldiers trained for war, Vasiko engaged in a spiritual battle. Despite the rigorous discipline and the watchful eyes of political officers, he adhered to a rigorous fast. A challenging endeavor in a mess hall that made no accommodations for religious dietary laws. When meat was served in the mess hall, he would refuse it, citing severe stomach pains to avoid suspicion. However, his most significant act of defiance was his commitment to liturgical life.

He discovered the functioning St. Nicholas Church in

Batumi and, in defiance of regulations and risking court-martial, would sneak away from his unit to attend services. There, concealed among the few daring babushkas and believers, the Soviet soldier received the Holy Mysteries, while partaking of the Body and Blood of Christ. Though he wore a soldier's uniform, his spirit was that of a monk.

By God's mercy, he was eventually assigned to deliver mail. This role afforded him a degree of freedom and mobility that allowed him to balance his military duties with his clandestine church attendance. He served not as a soldier of the Kremlin, but as a soldier of Christ behind enemy lines.

The Backyard Cathedral

Upon his return, Vasiko embarked on a project that would define his early adulthood. In the courtyard of his family home, he began constructing a church with his own hands.

This was the height of the atheistic purges, a period when people, driven by fear or lost faith, were discarding their icons. Holy images were cast into attics, basements, and, most commonly, city dumps. Vasiko became a scavenger of the sacred, spending days sifting through refuse in search of discarded icons. When he found an icon—often dirty, broken, or desecrated—he would rescue it. He established a small workshop in his home, where he cleaned the images and fashioned new frames from various materials, occasionally repurposing tin from sardine cans. He adorned the walls of his modest sanctuary with these rescued saints, creating a space that one American pilgrim later described as an "Orthodox Disneyland" due to its dense, vibrant, and multicolored collection of holy images.

The construction of a church in a private yard did not go unnoticed by the communist authorities, who reacted with outrage. Government officials attempted to demolish the building, but they encountered unexpected resistance. On one occasion, a group of officials arrived to enforce the demolition. Before they could announce their intentions, Father Gabriel, as he would later be known, preemptively declared, "I will not destroy the church, if you can, try...".

When workers arrived to carry out the demolition, he threatened them with spiritual authority, warning, "Remember, the one who gives orders will be punished more than the one who executes." Intimidated by his boldness and perhaps by a lingering fear of divine retribution, the workers fled.

Nevertheless, the pressure remained unrelenting. At one point, the regime forced the demolition of the church. His sister, Julietta, recalled the profound anguish this caused him, witnessing him kneeling in the ruins, crying out, "My Lord, how can I destroy the church dedicated to you?" Yet, he remained undeterred, rebuilding the church three separate times. Eventually, the head of the Soviet police and the secretary of the district party committee came to him discreetly to offer a personal pardon. He restored the chapel, changing its design from seven cupolas to a single large central dome, a structure that stands to this day.

The Path to the Altar

Vasiko's fervor attracted the attention of the highest authority in the Georgian Church, Catholicos-Patriarch Melchizedek III. With the Patriarch's blessing, Vasiko began serving at Sioni Cathedral, initially as a watchman and subsequently as a reader.

His childhood desire for monasticism evolved into an all-consuming passion. He petitioned the Bishop of Kutaisi, Gabriel (Chachanidze), stating, "Since childhood, I have had a firm decision to serve our Holy Mother Church... I ask you humbly... to be ordained."

On January 25, 1955, he submitted another petition requesting to be appointed as an unsalaried deacon, citing his disability status. His request was granted January 30, 1955, and he was consecrated as a deacon.

That same day, Father Gabriel wrote an "oath list" and a "humble request":

I, Goderzi Urgebadze, being appealed to serve a clerical pay my vows and make solemn affirmation with appeal unto the Lord, Almighty, the Gospel and Life-Giving Cross — wish to pass services of God, The Holy Word of God according to church canons and give a pledge to perform Divine Liturgies strictly in accordance with the adopted church canons and no alterations, to defend teachings of holy fathers and Orthodox church on the basis of deep faith and convey them to the laity; protest the souls of the flock entrusted from the heresies and schism entrusted and avert from hostilities those averted into schisma and direct them towards the road of truth; deny myself by filling my life with renewed spirit and clear consciousness, avert worldly charms humbly with calmness and through God-pleasing deeds and enlighten fellow men to seed goodness; neither personal benefits nor reverences but glorify God, strengthening the church and encouraging the neighbor.

I through intercession of the Mgost Holy Mother of God and All Saints may God, our Lord grant me Divine Grace. In support of a pledge I kiss the Gospel and the Holy Cross of our Savior. Amen.

Since my childhood, my cherished hope has been to serve God and lead a monastic life, that is why I ask you kindly to accept my humble request to be ordained with little schema and give me the name of Saint Gabriel the Anthonite.

The request was gratified by Bishop Gabriel and addressed to Archimandrite George:

"Bestow a blessing on the schema, receive the deacon's confession and give him the name of the reverend Saint Gabriel the Anthonite, according to his will"

Finally, the day arrived for him to leave the world behind completely. On February 23, 1955, at the Motsameta Monastery in Kutaisi, Deacon Goderdzi was tonsured into the small schema. He was given the name Gabriel in honor of Saint Gabriel the Athonite, the monk who had walked upon the sea to retrieve the Iveron Icon of the Mother of God.

Three days later, at the Saints Peter and Paul Cathedral, Bishop Gabriel ordained him as a hieromonk. The boy who had built churches out of matchboxes was now a priest of the Most High God.

Service and Sorrow

From the moment of his tonsure, Hieromonk Gabriel dedicated himself to service with remarkable zeal. He initially served at Sioni Cathedral and, from 1960, at his beloved Bethany Monastery.

Bethany was a spiritual oasis, home to his mentors, Father George (Mkheidze) and Father John (Maisuradze). He labored alongside these holy men, whom he loved deeply. However, the Soviet government was determined to suppress this remnant of monastic life. In 1962, following the deaths of Father John, Father George, and the priest-monk Vasili, the government ordered the closure of Bethany Monastery.

Forced to leave his spiritual home, Father Gabriel returned to Tbilisi, where he served at the Trinity Cathedral of All Saints from 1962 to 1965, gathering a small parish around him. However, the fire burning within him could not be contained within the walls of a parish church. As the Soviet regime grew increasingly oppressive, Father Gabriel prepared for an act of confession that would irrevocably alter his life and transform him into a living martyr. The time of quiet building had ended; the time of the fire was approaching.

Chapter 4

Fire on Rustaveli Avenue

"Death is transfiguration. Don't be afraid of death; rather, be afraid of the Judgement Day."

The Red Feast

The date was May 1, 1965. In the Soviet Union, this day marked compulsory celebration—International Workers' Day. It was a significant occasion in the liturgical calendar of the communist state, characterized by a festival of red flags, marching bands, and the rhythmic, thundering boots of the proletariat marching in unison. Tbilisi, the capital of the Georgian Soviet Socialist Republic, had been transformed into a temple of ideology. The central thoroughfare, Rustaveli Avenue, was meticulously cleaned and adorned, prepared to receive the adoration of the masses.

However, for Hieromonk Gabriel, the atmosphere of the city was not one of celebration, but rather one of suffocation. The air was thick with a worship that did not belong to God. According to some accounts, this day of secular pomp coincided with Holy Saturday, the most solemn day of the Orthodox year, when Christ lies in the tomb and the faithful await the Resurrection. Father Gabriel had just returned from serving the Divine Liturgy, his heart filled with the bloodless sacrifice of the altar, only to step out into a world consumed by the worship of a dead man.

The focal point of the demonstration was the building of the Council of Ministers (the Supreme Council) on Rustaveli Avenue. To commemorate the occasion, party officials had erected a monument to their idol: a colossal portrait of Vladimir Lenin. The dimensions of this image were staggering; sources describe it as twelve meters high (nearly forty feet), a banner stretching two stories tall, covering the façade of the government building. It depicted the leader of the revolution in full figure, gazing down upon the Georgians with the stern benevolence of a totalitarian father. Above or below the image, the caption blazed in bold letters: "Glory to Great Lenin!"

Government speakers stood at the rostrum, delivering speeches that extolled the virtues of the regime, their voices amplified across the square packed with thousands of people. It was the peak of the demonstration. The crowd remained frozen in the passive reverence demanded by the state. Yet high above them, unnoticed by the guards or the secret police, a small figure in a black cassock had gained entrance to the building.

The Act of War

Father Gabriel had meticulously prepared for this moment. He entered the attic of the Executive Committee building earlier, positioning himself in the dust and darkness, awaiting the commencement of the demonstration. He was armed not with a weapon of steel, but with a weapon of light—and a jug of kerosene.

He found a window on the second floor that gave him access to the rear of the massive canvas. The portrait was vast, a wall of cloth blocking out the sun. With quiet determination, the monk poured kerosene over the back of the portrait, thoroughly soaking the fabric in preparation for a transformation. Then, with a prayer that resembled more of a battle cry than a whisper, he struck a match.

The fire ignited instantly. Kerosene is unforgiving, and the flames raced up the twelve-meter expanse of the dictator's image with a deafening roar.

Down in the square, the drone of political speeches was suddenly interrupted by a gasp that reverberated through the crowd. The face of Lenin, the "god" of the Soviet Union, was disintegrating. The portrait erupted into a sheet of fire. The flames consumed the cloth, curling the painted edges of the leader's coat and face, transforming the symbol of eternal communist power into black smoke and ash.

Horror swept over the square. The thousands of people gathered there froze. The music stopped. The speeches died in the throats of the officials. A paralyzing stillness descended upon Tbilisi. It was an unimaginable sight—the burning of the idol in the very heart of the empire's power.

The Sermon from the Window

However, the fire was merely the beginning. As the portrait blazed, creating a frame of fire around him, Father Gabriel emerged at the second-floor window. He did not hide. He did not flee. He stood framed by the destruction he had caused, gazing down at the sea of terrified faces.

He began to preach.

His voice, empowered by the Holy Spirit and the adrenaline of martyrdom, resonated throughout the square. He called out to the crowd, delivering a sermon that struck at the very root of their fear and idolatry.

"The Lord said, 'Thou shalt not make unto thee idols or any graven images... Thou shalt not bow down before them nor serve them, for I am the Lord your God. Thou shalt have no other gods!'" he proclaimed, quoting the book of Exodus.

The crowd gazed up, dumbfounded. The audacity of the moment was paralyzing. A monk, a remnant of what some considered the "backward" past, was dismantling the present reality.

"People, come to your senses!" Gabriel cried out. "The Georgians have always been Christians! So why are you bowing down before idols?"

He pointed to the burning effigy, the charred remains of Lenin now falling like black snow. "Glory is not due to this corpse, but to Jesus Christ!" he shouted. "Why are you bowing down before idols? Glory is due not to this corpse but to Jesus Christ, Who trampled down death and gave us eternal life!"

He continued his condemnation of their false worship: "Jesus Christ died and rose again... But your cast idols will never be resurrected. Even during their life, they were dead..."

It was a scene of biblical proportions—a new Elijah mocking the prophets of Baal, a moment akin to the Three Holy Youths in the fiery furnace of Soviet Georgia. For a few seconds, the truth hung in the air, undeniable and terrifying.

The Passion of the Confessor

The paralysis of the crowd shattered. The state machinery, momentarily stunned, roared back to life with violent fury. The doors of the Executive Committee building had been locked, but the authorities mobilized quickly. Fire engines were brought in, and ladders were raised to the second floor to apprehend the "enemy of the people."

They dragged Father Gabriel down from his fiery pulpit. However, they did not arrest him in a civil manner. As soon as he touched the ground, the mob descended upon him. The "people," whose liberation the regime claimed to champion, transformed into a pack of wolves. They broke through the barricades, driven by a mix of ideological rage and a primal instinct to destroy what they feared.

The beating was savage. They kicked him with heavy boots, assaulted him with the butts of their rifles, and doused him with fire hoses. The air resonated with screams of hatred: "Let me finish off that louse!" Each person wanted to trample him underfoot, eager to demonstrate their loyalty to the burning idol by destroying the man who had lit the match.

Father Gabriel did not resist. He accepted the blows as participation in the suffering of the Savior he had just proclaimed. The violence was so extreme that it was a miracle he was not torn to pieces on the pavement. He sustained seventeen fractures to his skull and body, a broken jaw, and his face was reduced to a "bloody mess" that was unrecognizable.

He was spared from immediate death only through the intervention of the notorious 8th Regiment. The authorities, recognizing that a public lynching could elevate the "madman" to martyrdom or simply needing him alive to uncover the "conspiracy," extracted his broken body from the mob. A "level one alarm"—the highest state of emergency in the Soviet Union—was declared in the city. The regime was alarmed, believing this could not be the act of a solitary individual; it had to be a signal for an uprising.

The Interrogation

Father Gabriel was taken to the isolation cell of the Georgian KGB (Security Department) hospital. He lay there, gravely injured, teetering on the brink of death for nearly a month. He was treated with care, not out of compassion, but because the authorities required him to be coherent. They were preparing a show trial and needed a confession.

The interrogation was merciless. The communist authorities were convinced that this was a coordinated plot by the Georgian Orthodox Church. They demanded that Gabriel confess to a conspiracy and promised him clemency if he would implicate the Church hierarchy.

"Confess," they insisted. "Tell us who orchestrated this. Name the conspirators, and we will spare you."

Yet, the monk, physically broken, remained unyielding in spirit. He refused to implicate anyone, asserting that the act was solely his, born from his conscience and duty to God.

When asked again about his motivations, and expecting a political manifesto, he provided a theological one. "I did it because it is forbidden to treat a man like God," he explained to his interrogators. "The Crucifixion of Christ ought to hang where the portrait of Lenin was. And you need to write, 'Glory to the Lord Jesus Christ.'"

Frustrated by his obstinacy, the interrogators attempted to intimidate him. They praised Lenin and demanded respect for the founder of the state.

Father Gabriel, gazing at them through his swollen eyes, uttered a sentence that sealed his fate as a madman in their eyes, but as a confessor in the eyes of Heaven. He called Lenin a "beast."

For this, he was beaten again, severely. The threat of execution loomed over him, and the investigation was treated as a mere formality to justify the bullet.

The Scandal to the World

Seventeen fractures, a broken jaw, and a skull cracked by the fury of the mob—this was the price of the sermon he had delivered from the burning window of the Council of Ministers. Under normal circumstances, in the ruthless calculus of the Soviet regime, a man who burned a twelve-meter portrait of Lenin during a May Day parade would simply disappear. A bullet to the back of the neck in a dark cellar was the standard prescription for such brazen counter-revolutionary agitation.

However, the Soviet Union in 1965 was not the same as it had been in 1937. And the regime found itself in a delicate geopolitical bind. The Iron Curtain was not soundproof.

The story of the monk who burned Lenin's portrait and preached Christ from the window of the Council of Ministers leaked out. The image of the burning "god" of Communism and the monk who dared to preach Christ over the flames had leaked to the international press, appearing in European and American magazines.

The Kremlin found itself in a precarious position. Executing a monk for a religious protest would result in a public relations disaster, confirming to the world the brutal persecution of religion that they publicly denied. They needed a way to neutralize Gabriel without making him a martyr.

The solution was the favorite weapon of the late Soviet state: punitive psychiatry. If Gabriel was not a political revolutionary, he must be insane. After all, in the logic of scientific atheism, who but a madman would risk his life for a God who did not exist? Who but a psychopath would burn the image of the great Lenin?

In August 1965, the Supreme Court of Georgia commuted his death sentence. Instead of the firing squad, Father Gabriel was ordered to be transferred to a psychiatric hospital for a "court-ordered psychopathic evaluation." indefinitely.

The state decided that it was better to brand him a lunatic than to acknowledge him as a confessor.

Diagnosis #666

On August 18, 1965, the prisoner listed as "Vassili Urge-badze" was admitted to the Tbilisi City Psycho-Neurological

Hospital at 1 Electroni Street. He was listed as being born in 1929, with a sixth grade education.

What followed was a bureaucratic attempt to pathologize holiness. The medical conclusion generated by the Soviet doctors is one of the most extraordinary documents in the history of hagiography. Intended to condemn him, it instead reads like a canonical verification of his saintliness, written by the very enemies of the faith.

The documentation of this "condition" was presented with bureaucratic precision. The doctors, acting as agents of state ideology, questioned him about his childhood visions—specifically, the encounter with the demon at age twelve. They recorded his belief that all evil in the world was attributable to sinister forces. But the evidence listed to support this diagnosis was nothing less than a description of a perfect monk. The doctors noted with clinical detachment:

"The patient contends that all the evils in the world are the result of malevolent forces. He began attending churches, engaging in prayer, acquiring icons, and studying church literature from the age of 12... He observed fasting on Wednesdays and Fridays."

The report detailed how adults and soldiers had ridiculed him for his fasting, laughing at his "nonsense" that Judas sold Christ on Wednesday and the Jews crucified Him on Friday. To the Soviet psychiatrists, this historical adherence to Church tradition was evidence of "hallucinations."

They observed him in isolation. They noted that he "mutters to himself in a low voice," a clear reference to the unceasing Jesus Prayer, which they interpreted as "whispered self-talk." They wrote that he "believes in the existence of heavenly beings, God, and angels." Perhaps most telling of all, the doctors complained that his worldview was immovable: "The main axis of a psychopath is always directed towards the claim that everything is by God's will."

The report indicated that he was "disoriented in time, place, and environment"—a common medical characterization of holy fools who exist within the timeline of the Kingdom rather than that of the world.

The verdict from the Soviet psychiatrists was swift and politically expedient: "Psychopathic personality inclined to psychotic fits similar to schizophrenia."

However, one detail in the documentation sent a chill through the faithful who later saw it. The official medical card, the document that branded him a madman and spared him from the firing squad, bore a specific registration number.

It was number **666**.

Whether by demonic coincidence or divine irony, the confessor who had denounced the image of the antichristian power was marked with the number of the Beast. It was a stamp of the enemy that Father Gabriel would wear as a badge of honor, signifying his complete alienation from the system that governed the world.

The White Ticket

Father Gabriel spent seven months in the psychiatric hospital, a place rife with horror, where political dissidents and individuals with genuine mental health issues were intermingled and subjected to abuse. Where powerful drugs like aminazine were used to break the will. Yet, even here, God preserved him.

Even in this environment, surrounded by the truly mentally ill, Gabriel remained an evangelist. The doctors noted with frustration: "When engaged in conversation, he surely mentioned God, angels, and icons." He was entirely "uncritical of his condition," meaning he refused to admit that his faith was a disease.

During this time, Gabriel established a parish. He formed connections with the mentally ill, providing them with the only comfort they had likely ever experienced.

The Soviet authorities intended to confine him indefinitely, labeling him a "hopeless case." But God's will intervened, working through the unlikely figure of the esteemed Georgian academician, A. Zurabashvili. The academician, perhaps sensing the spiritual depth behind the "madness" or simply recognizing the political embarrassment of the situation, advocated for his release.

It is a striking paradox that Soviet officials used the medical characterization of Father Gabriel's *virtuous life*—his fasting, prayer, and belief in angels—as the rationale for his discharge. They concluded that he was a "psychopathic individual who believes in God and angels," thus deeming him harmlessly insane.

On November 19, 1965, he was discharged and sent home to his mother, Barbara, on Tetri Tskaro Street. They issued a certificate declaring him "mentally ill." In the Soviet Union, this was referred to as a "White Ticket"—a document that exempted an individual from military service (retrospectively, in his case) and prohibited him from holding any official employment. The diagnosis served as a tool of the regime, intended to neutralize an individual whose consciousness posed a threat to the communist system.

He was granted a second-category disability pension. This was a gross violation of legal norms—had he truly been disabled, he should never have been conscripted—but logic was of little concern to the regime. They labeled him insane, believing that only a madman would have faith in God, angels, and demons. He was granted a second-category disability pension of seventeen rubles per month.

The Martyrdom of Silence

Father Gabriel walked out of the asylum alive, but he did not enter into freedom; instead, he stepped into a different form of martyrdom.

The Soviet authorities imposed a condition on his release: the Church hierarchy was to suspend him from his priestly ministry. The Patriarchate, under immense pressure and striving to survive the hostile regime, acquiesced. Consequently, Father Gabriel was suspended, forbidden from serving the Liturgy or entering the altar.

This was a blow far heavier than the rifle butts on Rustaveli Avenue. For a man who lived for the Eucharist and had built a church with his own hands, being barred from the service of God constituted profound spiritual agony.

He became a pariah. His former friends and fellow priests avoided him, fearing association with the "crazy" monk who had challenged the state. Neighbors would unleash their dogs upon him if he was seen during the day. The man who, as a child, had been so gentle that he refused to use mousetraps was now hunted like an animal in his own street.

He and his mother lived in abject poverty on his meager pension. The seventeen rubles a month were barely enough to keep them both alive. For ten years, he existed on the fringes of society.

In an effort to appease the authorities and perhaps to protect the Church, he was not even allowed to receive Holy Communion as a priest. Instead, he stood in line with the laity, head bowed, receiving the Mysteries as a simple sinner.

He often retreated to his church in the backyard, weeping uncontrollably.

"Vasiko, brother, why are you crying? Is anything wrong with you?" she would ask, entering the small sanctuary to find him in tears.

He would look at her with eyes full of sorrow and reply, "Christ was born in a manger; but people respect me and kiss me on the hand."

This cryptic answer revealed the depth of his internal struggle. He was torn between the profound humility of Christ, who was born in poverty and rejection, and the reverence people had once shown him as a priest—a reverence that was now stripped away, leaving him exposed to the mockery of the world. He was learning, through brutal experience, that the path to Christ leads inevitably to Golgotha.

For years, he struggled to secure employment. He moved between villages, occasionally hired to guard vineyards or tend fires in churches, always on the periphery, constantly observed, labeled as the "psychopath" with the White Ticket.

Eventually, the trauma took its toll on his mother, Barbara. She became paralyzed, unable to move or work. Now, Father Gabriel could no longer wander to find work; he was tethered to his home to care for her. To survive, the confessor of the faith was reduced to begging. For several years, he could be found sitting at the portico of some church, his hand outstretched, asking for alms. Only strangers would give him anything; his acquaintances, seeing the fallen priest, would turn away in shame or disgust.

The fire on Rustaveli Avenue not only consumed the portrait of Lenin but also incinerated Father Gabriel's identity as a "respectable" clergyman. Although he survived the blaze, it irrevocably altered him. From the ashes of the dignified

Hieromonk Gabriel emerged something entirely different—something wilder, more peculiar, and infinitely more powerful. The Confessor was no longer part of the world; the *Salos*—the Fool for Christ—was born.

Chapter 5

Birth of the Salos

"To become wise, first, you must be stupid."

Backyard Demolition

Even in his exile, the Soviet authorities could not leave him in peace. The church he had built in his yard on Tetri Tskaro Street remained a thorn in their side—a visible symbol of defiance.

The order came down to demolish it. A high-ranking church hierarch, under pressure from the Commissioner for Religious Affairs, came to Father Gabriel's house. The Commissioner waited outside, representing the iron fist of the state, while the hierarch entered the room where Gabriel was praying.

"Gabriel, my son," the hierarch said, likely with a heavy heart. "You have built a wonderful church with your own hands. But do you not know that we are living in difficult times? Listen, my son. Take it apart. Better times will come.

The situation will change, and you will build the church again. Tell the Commissioner that you will do as I say."

It was a test of obedience. Father Gabriel did not argue. He did not scream about his rights or the sanctity of the place. He went outside to the Commissioner and said simply, "I will take the church apart."

The officials left, satisfied. They had broken the monk's will —or so they thought.

A few days later, Father Gabriel began his work. He dismantled the front wall of the church. But he did not destroy it. He moved the wall two meters *forward* and rebuilt it, making the church even larger than it was before.

When the authorities returned, stunned by his audacity, he told them, "I listened and did what I was told. Now that better times have come, I have rebuilt the church again."

Amazingly, they left him alone. Perhaps they decided he was truly too crazy to reason with, or perhaps they feared the undeniable power that radiated from this broken man. He had rebuilt the church three separate times after various attempts to destroy it. Eventually, even the head of the Soviet police and the secretary of the district party committee came to him secretly, offering personal apologies. The church stood—a testament to the fact that while they could break his body, they could not break his spirit.

The Birth of the Salos

It was during these dark years of ostracism and persecution that the final transformation of Father Gabriel took place. The dignified Hieromonk Gabriel died, and the *Salos*—the Fool-for-Christ—was born.

He realized that to survive and to continue his mission, he had to hide his sanctity completely. He made a conscious, resolute decision to adopt the mask of insanity permanently. It was a strategy of spiritual camouflage. As he later explained, "When it seemed to me that I was an important person or that I was better than others, I would act that way (foolishly); and when people would laugh at me, I'd be humbled and see that I'm garbage."

He began to do things that shocked the pious and delighted the wicked. He, who had never touched alcohol, would now sit in the street with a jug of wine, feigning drunkenness. He would shout and preach loudly in public places, acting the part of the village idiot.

One day, he walked through the monastery courtyard where several priests were sitting on a bench. These were men who likely looked down on him, the "suspended" priest. Father Gabriel approached them and began to dance wildly, a grotesque parody of joy. The priests were horrified. They got up and fled from the "mad monk."

But they fled not just because he was embarrassing, but because he was exposing them. As one source reveals, the priests secretly knew *why* he was dancing: the day before, they had all taken off their cassocks, donned secular clothes, and gone dancing and drinking in a nightclub. Gabriel's "madness" was a mirror reflecting their own hidden sins.

This became his method. He used his "insanity" to say things no sane person would dare say. He denounced the authorities, rebuked the lax clergy, and humbled the proud, all while protected by the shield of his diagnosis. Who arrests a man who is already certified as crazy? Who takes offense at a drunkard?

Restoration

The exile lasted for nearly six years. It was a time of

refining fire. But in 1971, the thaw began. The Catholicos-Patriarch of All Georgia, Ephrem II, along with the future Patriarch Ilia II (who was then a Metropolitan and head of the seminary), decided that the punishment had lasted long enough.

They lifted the suspension. Father Gabriel was restored to his priestly ministry. He was appointed as the priest of the Samtavro Convent and Seminary in Mtskheta. He was given a cell in the Old King Mirian Tower for his permanent residence.

It was a moment of vindication, but Father Gabriel did not return to "normalcy." He accepted the tower with joy, saying, "Through the mercy of Our Savior and Our Lady, and with the blessings of two patriarchs, I have been bestowed with this cell." But he brought the *Salos* with him. He moved into the tower, but he also took up residence in a chicken coop. He wore the vestments of a priest, but he continued to wear the mask of the fool.

The Confessor had survived the fire and the asylum. Now, the Elder was ready to begin his strangest and most beautiful work: saving souls by acting like he had lost his mind.

Chapter 6

The Mask of Foolishness

"A humbled man is protected from temptations. No one can enter the Kingdom of God without humbleness."

The Professor

By the early 1970s, Father Gabriel had settled into a life rhythm that was both perplexing and sacred. Having endured the turmoil of the 1965 demonstration and the confines of a psychiatric ward, he now walked the streets of Mtskheta and Tbilisi, safeguarded by the very document intended to undermine him: the "White Ticket." The Soviet regime had labeled him a madman, a designation Father Gabriel chose to embrace not out of insanity, but as part of a deliberate spiritual strategy known in the Orthodox tradition as *Salos*, or Fool-for-Christ. To conceal his spiritual gifts and avoid the toxicity of worldly acclaim, he adopted a persona of eccentricity that he maintained until his final days.

Among his most common props in this performance of humility was a bottle of red wine. To the untrained observer, the Elder appeared to be a drunkard. He would often be seen sitting on the street or outside his cell with a jug of wine, sometimes staggering or shouting, provoking scandal among the devout and affirming the suspicions of the judgmental. He affectionately referred to the wine as "The Professor." When he received guests, he would frequently call out to the nuns, "Bring the Professor!" and pour glasses for everyone, blessing them to drink "to the bottom" (or *do dna* in Russian), while he himself often abstained or merely feigned taking a sip.

On one notable occasion, during the solemn period of Great Lent, he astonished the nuns and parishioners at the Samtavro Convent by bursting into the church, exclaiming, "The cats have stolen my sausage!" The congregation, adhering strictly to their Lenten fast and abstaining from meat, were taken aback by their priest's lament over a lost sausage during this sacred time. However, those with spiritual discernment recognized the underlying lesson: he was critiquing their legalism, illustrating that "it is not what goes into a person's mouth that makes him ritually unclean; rather, what comes out of it."

His behavior during the Pascha (Easter) celebration was equally shocking to those unfamiliar with him. The future Metropolitan Isaiah, then a young student, recalled his first encounter with Father Gabriel on Easter. The Elder, adorned with a distinctive head covering, summoned the young man, filled a glass with the "Professor," and instructed, "You have to drink it... God has forgiven all our sins; now we can drink a little and rejoice. Who is thinking about sin today is worse than Judas." Later that evening, during the service, Father Gabriel ascended the *amvon* (the space in front of the altar) to deliver a sermon. He spoke with compelling gestures, referencing movie stars and directors. Then, lifting his hands and eyes to heaven, he unexpectedly slipped off the *amvon* and collapsed onto the floor. Visitors from Tbilisi expressed indignation at the "clumsy" monk, but the young Isaiah felt joy, recognizing that the Elder was purposefully relinquishing his dignity to emphasize the joy of the Resurrection.

The Hen House and the Tower

In 1971, Father Gabriel was appointed as the priest of the Samtavro Convent and Seminary. The Patriarchate granted him the use of the ancient King Mirian Tower as his residence, a structure dating back to the 4th century. He often expressed genuine joy, stating, "Through the mercy of Our Savior and Our Lady... I have been bestowed with this cell." However, the *Salos* within him favored a more modest dwelling.

In 1987, he opted for a small wooden shed located in a corner of the monastery yard, known as *Kaklovani* (the walnut alley). This shed had previously served as a hen house. It was a diminutive, drafty structure with gaps in the wooden walls measuring two to three centimeters wide. During the harsh winter frost in Mtskheta, the wind would whistle through these openings, yet the Elder steadfastly refused to use heating. He often slept there, at times curled up in the confined space where one could barely stand upright.

When the novice Theodora, who would later become an abbess, first arrived at the convent, Father Gabriel issued a strict warning to the nuns: "Here the monk Gabriel will reside, and nobody dares to enter it, none of you." Despite this admonition, Theodora and another nun chose to clean the coop to prepare it for him. While they were scrubbing the filth, the Elder appeared. Rather than respond with the anger they anticipated, he expressed approval of their dedication and blessed them. For a period, he resided in that coop, and the nuns observed in awe as he walked barefoot through the snow during the depths of winter, seemingly unaffected by the cold. This was a remarkable demonstration of asceticism, cloaked in the guise of poverty and madness.

The School of Humility

Life with Father Gabriel was a continuous trial by fire. He regarded himself as "garbage" and a "worm," and he was resolute in his mission to lead those around him to that same blessed state of profound humility. His approach was not one of gentle persuasion; he employed shock therapy.

He frequently shouted at the nuns, using derogatory names or chasing them away to test their obedience. On one occasion, he locked the door of the refectory after a meal and refused to allow the nuns to leave. He instructed the future abbess, Ketevan, to fetch a bowl and wash the hands of all the sisters. When she returned with the bowl filled with dirty, soapy water, he fixed her with a piercing gaze and commanded, "Drink the water to the last drop." To the astonishment of the others, she complied without hesitation. He then embraced her affectionately and blessed her; this was a test of her willingness to serve.

He had a distinctive method of addressing the nuns to assess their pride. He referred to one nun as "Chanticleer" (a rooster), repeating the name until she exited the room in tears. On another occasion, he observed a nun who appeared excessively proud of her prayerful demeanor. He mimicked the sound of a machine gun—"Tra-ta-ta-ta!"—and exclaimed, "What is it? Are you saying prayers or reading a newspaper?! It sounds like shooting with Chapaev's machine gun."

His methods were equally stringent with the laity. On one occasion, two women brought him homemade pastries when they learned he was ill. Father Gabriel, who was resting, abruptly rose and exclaimed, "How dare you touch me, a monk? Are you attempting to seduce me? Leave immediately, both of you, and do not forget to take your pastries with you!" The women, terrified, fell to their knees. He remained adamant until they left, trembling. As soon as the door closed, the "angry" Elder began to pray for them with fervent love, blessing them and their families. He turned to a witness and smiled, saying, "Their visit to a monk was not revered, but they will learn now how to behave with clerics."

Even the clergy were not exempt from his lessons. During the Divine Liturgy, he once performed somersaults within the church, rolling around on the floor. The congregation was scandalized, but a group of young men later discerned the truth: the Elder was diverting attention from the priests who were judging him, or perhaps he was mocking the world's inverted priorities. On another occasion, he saw a priest walking with an air of arrogance. Father Gabriel approached him and shouted vulgar, abusive words. When the priest stopped and humbly replied, "I'm much worse than that, Father Gabriel," the Elder immediately embraced him and said, "You are my brother."

The Flying Cement

While Father Gabriel went to great lengths to conceal his sanctity, the veil between the physical and spiritual realms often grew thin around him. One of the most extraordinary miracles, which he strictly commanded to remain confidential until his death, was witnessed by his sister, Julietta.

During the construction of his church in the backyard of his family home, Father Gabriel was working alone. The task was labor-intensive, involving the mixing and transporting of concrete to the upper sections of the walls. Julietta came to visit him and found the gate locked. Father Gabriel opened it, but he was in a hurry. "Sister," he said, "I don't have any time to interrupt my work, and I'm hungry. Please bring me a bottle of Georgian yogurt."

He handed her the money and the keys, adding a peculiar instruction: "I will continue my work. Lock the gate from the outside, and when you return, be sure to call me BEFORE you open the gate."

Julietta went to fetch the yogurt and encountered a milkman nearby. In her haste and joy to return quickly, she overlooked her brother's specific instruction. She unlocked the gate without calling out and entered the courtyard.

She froze at the sight before her, which defied the laws of physics. Buckets filled with wet cement flew through the air on their own, ascending from the ground to the top of the church walls. They emptied themselves into the frames prepared for construction before descending again. Father Gabriel stood in the courtyard below, kneading the cement and pouring it into the buckets, yet he was not carrying them. The buckets moved as if they were on "magic carpets."

Upon her entry, the Elder noticed her and realized she had witnessed the miracle. Initially, he was angry at her disobedience, admonishing her for entering without warning. However, upon seeing her shock, he calmed her and made her promise, at that moment, not to disclose what she had seen. "Haven't I asked her not to tell this story to anyone?" he would later say when the story leaked out. "I have nothing to do with this. I was working alone, and when it became very difficult, God took pity on me!" Julietta kept this secret for over thirty years, only revealing it after the saint's repose.

The Diadem and the Crown of Thorns

Among his many eccentricities, Father Gabriel possessed a

literal crown. It was a copper diadem, sometimes described as being made from the neck of a broken pitcher or simple metal, which he would wear on his head. He would walk through the streets or appear at the tower door adorned with this "royal" headpiece.

When Patriarch Ilia II visited the monastery, Father Gabriel appeared wearing this diadem. The Patriarch, recognizing the Elder's spirit, inquired whether the diadem was made of gold. "No, Your Holiness," Gabriel answered. "Should it be golden, I would have been beheaded." This statement profoundly contrasted the nature of earthly power with spiritual kingship; he wore a crown of folly that was safe, whereas a crown of gold would bring death.

But he also possessed a crown of thorns, which he had fashioned himself with sharp spikes. He told the nuns, "Sometimes I put this wreath on my head, and when spikes pierce my head, I feel how our Saviour suffered." This private act of self-torture served as a counterbalance to his public persona of "drunkenness." While the world mocked the "crazy monk" with the wine bottle, he was in his cell, bleeding from the thorns and weeping for the sins of the world.

The Assault on Jvari

Father Gabriel's "foolishness" often functioned as a weapon against the pride of others. He had a spiritual daughter named Elizabeth (later known as Nun Elizabeth) whom he frequently tested. One Saturday morning, he announced to her, "Let's assault the Jvari Monastery!"

He blessed her to buy a bottle of vodka, which he concealed under his mantle. With a serious face, marched to the renowned monastery overlooking Mtskheta. Once there, in full view of the pilgrims and tourists, he opened the bottle, took a swig, and passed it to Elizabeth. She was horrified but complied. To her astonishment, when she drank, she tasted only water.

He then offered the bottle to those around him, playing the part of the merry drunkard. He turned to Elizabeth and commented, "Look, nobody blamed me; they all will reach the Heavenly Kingdom." He was illustrating to her that pure hearts do not judge. But the lesson was not over. He turned to her with a serious expression and said, "Sit down, extend your hand, and beg alms."

For a proud young woman, this was a mortifying ordeal. She sat and begged until sufficient money was collected. Father Gabriel then took the money and invited everyone nearby to a feast, serving the pilgrims while he himself abstained from food. He concluded this unusual "assault" with the teaching: "Everyone who humbles himself will be exalted."

The Theatre of the Unseen

Father Gabriel's cell was a space where the veil was continually lifted. He permitted his cell attendant, Nun Paraskeva, to enter without the customary prayer, merely by making the sign of the cross. One day, she entered and found him speaking animatedly to an empty room.

"Whom are you talking to?" she asked, seeing no one. "To angels," he replied simply.

On a separate occasion, he ordered Paraskeva to leave him alone because "I'm not to be watched." As she moved toward the door, she glanced back and saw his face "shining like the sun."

He also claimed to visit other places without leaving his bed. During a period of serious illness when he was bedridden, he told Paraskeva, "Now I'm going to Shavnabada Monastery."

She assumed he was joking. Later, he informed her that he had indeed been there, that everything was well, and that the Abbot was "counting the heads" of the monks.

A few days later, Archimandrite Shio, the abbot of Shavnabada, visited Samtavro. Paraskeva asked him, "How many are you in the monastery?" "I don't know!" the Abbot replied. "Some come, some go. I usually count them during meals." Father Gabriel looked at Paraskeva and smiled, having been present, invisibly observing the Abbot as he counted his flock.

"Score 1-0"

Even in casual encounters, his humor served as a trap for pride. On a rainy day, two sisters, Nata and Manana, met him in town. They were overjoyed to see him and sought his blessing. However, the ground was muddy, and they decided that, rather than kneeling as was customary with the Elder, they would simply bow slightly to avoid soiling their clothes.

Reading their thoughts, Father Gabriel promptly knelt down in the thick, wet mud. The sisters, shamed by his humility, had no choice but to kneel beside him in the muck. He blessed them there in the dirt, then winked at them and said, "Score 1-0!"

The Guardian of the Nation

Despite his antics, Father Gabriel was a staunch protector of his nation and faith. When armed men—members of the paramilitary groups destabilizing Georgia in the early 1990s—approached the convent, Father Gabriel did not hide. Instead, he boldly stepped out to confront them.

"What direction are you setting off, my sons?" he inquired. "To Zugdidi, to wage war," they replied. These were Georgians preparing to fight fellow Georgians in the civil war. "And whom are you going to wage war against, my brothers, they are Georgians, aren't they?"

He then raised his hands and shouted, "Shoot me! I am Georgia!" Grasping his crook, he swung it at them, declaring, "I will break your heads with this stick, you worthless cowards! You have to wear *lechaki* (a woman's headscarf), not caps!" The armed "knights," terrified by this raging monk who offered himself as a sacrifice, fled the church, nearly abandoning their weapons.

Whether he was feigning drunkenness with the "Professor," sleeping in a henhouse, or shouting at gunmen, Father Gabriel's seemingly foolish demeanor concealed a profound depth of love. He adopted an eccentric persona to prevent the world from idolizing him; yet, through his "madness," he compelled others to reflect on their own lives. As he once explained to a spiritual disciple: "When it seemed to me that I was an important person... I would act that way (foolishly); and when people would laugh at me, I'd be humbled and see that I'm garbage."

Chapter 7

The Clairvoyant

"Never betray God. Endure all trials, and the gates of the Heavens will be opened for you."

The Burden of Sight

By the 1980s, the ancient King Mirian Tower at Samtavro Convent had evolved from a mere residence for an eccentric monk into a spiritual observatory. As the Soviet Empire began to falter under the strain of stagnation, Father Gabriel occupied his round cell, encircled by icons that adorned the walls like a shimmering mosaic of witnesses. To the casual observer, he was still the eccentric with the "White Ticket," prone to outbursts or feigning drunkenness. But to those who dared to cross the threshold of his cell, it became unmistakably clear that Father Gabriel was not merely looking *at* them, but *through* them.

He possessed the gift of *kardiognosis*—the knowledge of hearts. This was not the vague intuition of a psychologist, but a precise, often surgical spiritual insight that dismantled every defense a person might construct. He knew the past that his visitors had forgotten and he saw the future that had not yet been written. As he once told a visitor who stood apprehensively outside his door, afraid to enter because she thought he was a prophet: "Who told you I am a prophet?! If you were afraid to come and still you have come!" He rejected the title but embodied its essence.

The Theology of Matter: The Hindu Visitor

Father Gabriel's clairvoyance was not limited to personal sins; it extended to the very essence of truth and dogma. He staunchly defended Orthodox theology, not with books or academic arguments, but with the raw power of God manifest in the physical realm.

One day, a Georgian man arrived at Samtavro. He was a seeker who had strayed far from the Orthodox path, immersing himself in Hinduism. After spending years in India, studying under a spiritual teacher, he returned with a worldview that perceived all religions as vague, interchangeable paths to the same truth. He came to debate, or perhaps merely to observe the "foolish" monk.

Father Gabriel did not engage him in a debate about the Upanishads or the Holy Fathers. Instead, he regarded the man with a gaze that brokered no argument. He picked up a piece of ordinary bread that was sitting on his table.

"Observe this and comprehend," the Elder instructed, making the sign of the Cross over the bread in the name of the Holy Trinity.

In an instant, the laws of physics collapsed. The bread in his hands disintegrated, transforming into its elemental components. Before the astonished gaze of the Hindu follower, the bread manifested as three distinct substances: water, wheat, and fire. The elements swirled together yet remained distinct, a physical embodiment of a mystery beyond human comprehension.

"Look at it and see," Father Gabriel commanded. "Just as it is with the Holy Trinity in its three hypostases – the Father, the Son, and the Holy Spirit."

The visitor stood transfixed, witnessing a miracle that resonated with the ancient traditions of the Desert Fathers, happening right there in a Soviet-occupied country. Father Gabriel then made the sign of the Cross over the elements a second time. The water, wheat, and fire converged once more, instantly reconstituting into a single piece of bread.

"As this bread is whole and cannot be divided," the Elder concluded, "so too is the Holy Trinity – one essence and indivisible." The visitor's intellectual constructs were shattered not by logic, but by a profound revelation of power.

"My Athos is Here"

Father Gabriel's spiritual insight also positioned him as a steadfast guardian of his nation's spiritual dignity. During this period, Georgia was emerging from seventy years of atheism, a nation spiritually battered and economically devastated. It was easy for outsiders to view the dilapidated churches and struggling faithful as indicators of a wasteland.

Archimandrite Joseph, the Abbot of the Xeropotamou Monastery on Mount Athos, visited Georgia with a delegation of Athonite monks. They traveled to the ancient capital of Mtskheta, visiting the Svetitskhoveli Cathedral and then the Samtavro Convent. The grandeur of the past starkly contrasted with the present's poverty. Overwhelmed by the challenging political and economic landscape, and perhaps perceiving the spiritual struggles of a nation recently liberated from an atheist regime, the distinguished Athonite Abbot felt a profound, silent regret. In the privacy of his own heart—voicing it to no one—he pondered: "Virgin Mary, you have abandoned Georgia!"

The delegation then went to receive the blessing of the "fool" in the tower. They approached Father Gabriel with the respect accorded to a local elder, anticipating a pious greeting. Instead, Father Gabriel confronted Father Joseph with sudden anger.

"How could you dare to boldly proclaim that the Virgin has 'abandoned Georgia'?" Gabriel thundered, exposing the Abbot's hidden thoughts to everyone present. "We are under the protection of the Holy Virgin through our prayers and her mercy, even if you fail to recognize it and disapprove!"

The Abbot was struck with horror. The thought had been hidden in the deepest recesses of his mind, yet this rag-clad monk had plucked it out as effortlessly as one might pull a book from a shelf. Father Joseph fell to his knees, seeking immediate forgiveness for his doubt.

Father Gabriel's anger dissipated as quickly as it had arisen. Observing the Abbot's humility, he warmly embraced the Greek guest and invited the delegation to his table. The Athonite monks, deeply moved by their encounter with a living saint, urged him to relocate to Mount Athos. They assured him that on the Holy Mountain, he would have everything he needed, surrounded by the greatest monastic tradition in the world.

Father Gabriel looked at them and gave an answer that has become legendary in Georgia. "I am here, on my Athos," he replied. "I would not trade my beloved Georgia for Athos."

The Magazine and the Safe

While he dealt with theological doubts through miracles, Father Gabriel dealt with moral failures through shock therapy. His method was to act out the sins of his visitors, humiliating himself to save them from their own secrets. Perhaps the most shocking example of his "foolishness" manifesting as clairvoyance involved a spiritual child named Otar Nikolaishvili.

Otar was a devoted follower, frequently driving the Elder to monasteries and spending time in his cell. However, Otar was living a double life, harboring a secret sin of lust that he had not confessed. One day, while Otar was visiting, Father Gabriel made a request that was so outrageous it left him utterly speechless.

"Go out," the Elder commanded, "and buy me a glamorous pornographic magazine." He added an absurd description, stating he wanted one that was "vigorous as a struggling fish."

Otar was taken aback. He stood there, blinking, unable to comprehend that his holy Elder was requesting something so disreputable. He refused, attempting to reason with Father Gabriel, but the Elder was adamant. He raised his voice, forcefully expelling Otar from the cell. "If you don't bring it, you will be punished very strictly!" he thundered.

Terrified by the Elder's anger and bewildered by the command, Otar obeyed. He left the monastery, located the objectionable publication, and returned. The reaction was swift and severe. The other monks in the brotherhood learned of Father Gabriel's request for pornography and began to denounce him, whispering about his "madness" and "immorality." Otar felt an overwhelming sense of guilt, believing he was responsible for tarnishing the Elder's reputation by complying with such a morally questionable request.

Suddenly, a realization struck Otar with the force of a revelation. His thoughts raced back to his office in Tbilisi, specifically to his safe—the heavy, locked box where he stored important documents. Hidden deep within that safe were compromising photographs of himself with two women, with a plate of fish visible on the table in the image.

The significance of this connection became clear. *The magazine. The fish. The scandal.* Father Gabriel was not requesting pornography for himself; rather, he was reflecting Otar's own hidden life. The Elder was shouldering the shame of "pornography," allowing the brotherhood to condemn *him* in order to compel Otar to confront the filth he had locked away.

Otar rushed to his office. He opened the safe, retrieved the photographs, and burned them until they were reduced to ash.

A few days later, for reasons unrelated to Otar, law enforcement agents arrived at his office to conduct a surprise search. They demanded he open his safe. Otar watched as they rifled through his documents. Had the photographs still been there, he would have faced public disgrace, scandal, and potential blackmail. The safe was empty. Father Gabriel, through his perceived "madness," had protected Otar from ruin, risking his own reputation to cleanse his spiritual charge.

The Unborn and the Hidden Thought

The Elder's cell was a place where the boundary between the spoken and the unspoken did not exist. Thoughts resonated within him as loudly as shouts.

A young married couple approached him to seek his counsel. The wife was pregnant. As they settled in the presence of the saint, Father Gabriel began to discuss the responsibilities associated with parenthood, addressing them with a serious demeanor.

"The baby hears everything," he cautioned. "Try to be always in good spirits and use kind words."

The husband, a man marked by modern skepticism, scoffed. "I don't hear what the neighbor is doing behind my wall," he countered. "How can the baby hear in the belly?"

Father Gabriel's eyes narrowed. "Don't you believe?" he asked. He then shifted his gaze to the mother's abdomen and spoke directly to the unborn child in a commanding tone.

"I'm asking you, the baby! Don't you hear the word of God?"

At that exact moment, the baby kicked. It was not a gentle flutter; the mother felt a vigorous and forceful kick that caused her to gasp and leave the room to compose herself. The father sat in stunned silence. The Elder had engaged with the fetus, and the fetus had responded.

This profound experience extended to the hidden ambitions and fears of the nuns who served him. Sister Thekla, then a novice, was grappling with the demanding schedule of monastic life. During midnight prayers, a barrage of dark thoughts assailed her mind. *Do you truly want to spend all your life rising at midnight?* the thoughts whispered. *You are so young, so beautiful. You are sacrificing your youth. Have you gone mad?*

She told no one. The following morning, she returned to her cell, exhausted and conflicted. On her way, she encountered Father Gabriel, who was in tears. He regarded her with profound compassion and began to articulate her thoughts, echoing them verbatim.

"So beautiful, so young!" he exclaimed, mocking the demons that had tormented her. "To rise at midnight, to pray... Are you truly going to stay here?"

Thekla was shocked. He was quoting her own internal monologue. A wave of shame washed over her, quickly replaced by relief. She realized she was not alone in her struggle; the Elder stood with her, fighting alongside her. The thoughts never troubled her with the same intensity again.

The Woman on the Lap

Perhaps the most notable demonstration of his clairvoyance involved a woman named Makvala. She was a woman of the world, dressed in trousers—considered immodest in the monastery—and adorned with heavy makeup. She had a reputation for leading a loose and sinful life.

One day, Father Gabriel was sitting on a bench in the convent courtyard when Makvala approached him. In a display of brazen disrespect and seductive intent, she sat directly on the monk's lap. She threw her arms around him and began kissing him on the cheek, cooing, "Father Gabriel, you are so handsome; I adore you, I want to come to you again."

The nuns stood frozen in horror. The sanctity of the monastery, the vow of chastity, and the dignity of the Elder were all being violated in this grotesque scene. They expected Father Gabriel to push her away, shout, or call down divine retribution.

He did none of those things. He remained still as a statue, his gaze fixed on the sky. He neither touched her nor recoiled. He simply endured her "affection" with a look of profound sorrow, as he listened to something the others could not hear: the desperate cry of a dying soul buried beneath layers of sin.

After a moment, he spoke softly. "Come, Makvala, come."

Hearing her name—which she had not given him—shook her. It was as though she had awakened from a trance. She jumped up, looked around at the stunned nuns with wide eyes, and ran out of the monastery.

The Elder immediately rose and retreated to his cell. He locked the door and requested that no one disturb him. For hours, on his knees, he implored the Holy Virgin to save Makvala's soul. He had foreseen the spiritual demise that awaited her, and he had accepted her shameful embrace to buy her time.

The following day, a woman returned to the convent. The nuns did not recognize her. She wore a long black skirt and a scarf covering her head, her face scrubbed clean of makeup. It was Makvala. She approached Father Gabriel's cell, weeping and wailing.

"Father Gabriel, I know you will not open the door, I know I will never see you again," she cried. "Please forgive my shameless behavior. I feel your power; you have raised me from death and changed my life."

She became a devoted Christian. The "scandal" had been a rescue operation.

The Sun and the Elements

Father Gabriel's communion with the spiritual world granted him dominion over the physical one. He appeared to exist in a reality in which the elements acknowledged his authority.

During the sweltering ~~of the~~ Georgian summer, visitors often found him sitting outside his cell under the intense sun. One man, unable to endure the heat, requested that the Elder move to the shade. Father Gabriel regarded him with confusion. He then turned his face upward, staring directly into the noon sun without blinking. He maintained this gaze for an extended period, his eyes wide open and unshielded.

"Is it so difficult to look at the sun?" he asked the man.

Then, lowering his gaze, he added quietly, "That's nothing. It's more difficult to contemplate the Creator of the Sun."

On another occasion, he exhibited an extraordinary control over machinery. He took a small chair and positioned himself in the midst of a busy street with heavy traffic. He began to preach and talk to pedestrians. While he remained seated, the traffic came to a standstill; not a single car passed by. The moment he rose and left, the cars returned, as if a dam had burst.

However, this power over nature was not always benevolent. It could manifest as a formidable judgment. One day, while preaching in the streets of Tbilisi, two teenagers mocked him. They ran up and snatched the pectoral reliquary cross from his chest—a sacred object containing relics. Father Gabriel called out to them, demanding the reliquary back. They returned it mockingly but retained the cross itself.

"The cross will judge you," Father Gabriel warned them sorrowfully. He refused to take the cross back from their hands.

A week later, a woman approached Father Gabriel to request a memorial service for one of the boys. Despite being in perfect health, the teenager who had stolen the cross had suddenly fallen ill and died. The Elder prayed for his soul, saving him from the abyss, but the lesson was clear: the holy things of God are not to be mocked.

The "Drunken" Prophet

To bear the weight of such knowledge—to witness the death of boys, the secret desires of men, and the hidden thoughts of abbots—was a burden too heavy for a normal man. To endure it, Father Gabriel retreated further into his "foolishness."

He would sit outside his cell with a jug of wine, covering it with a cloth as if attempting to conceal a vice, yet ensuring that everyone saw it. He feigned drunkenness to deter people from praising his miracles. When a hieromonk expressed disbelief in his miracles, Gabriel commanded him to kneel. The monk complied. "Now I bless you to rise," Gabriel said. The monk attempted to stand but found himself paralyzed, bound to the floor by an invisible force until the Elder released him.

On one occasion, a spiritual child named Nodar was driving Father Gabriel to Mtskheta when they were stopped by seven armed men—bandits who plagued Georgia during the lawless 1990s. They demanded the car. The situation was dire. Father Gabriel stepped out of the vehicle.

According to Nodar's testimony, something extraordinary occurred. It was as if a "huge glowing pillar descended from the sky." A supernaturally tall, handsome man with a white beard and a staff appeared—or perhaps Father Gabriel was transfigured into this form. He struck the ground with his staff and shouted in a voice that was not of this world: "How dare you stop us?! Shame on you!"

The armed bandits were overcome with terror. They dropped their weapons and fled in all directions. The one holding their documents froze, then thrust the papers back at Nodar, begging him to leave. They drove away in silence. Father Gabriel turned to Nodar, his face returning to its usual humble appearance.

"What do you say, Nodar?" he asked with a wink. "I think we did pretty well, didn't we?"

Whether transforming bread, reading minds, or instilling fear in bandits, Father Gabriel walked a delicate balance between two realms. He saw the angels and demons as clearly as he saw the trees and stones. As the 1990s descended into civil war and chaos, this vision would elevate him from a local eccentric to the weeping guardian of the nation. He began to ring the bells of Samtavro, proclaiming, "Blood! The blood of Georgians!" The Clairvoyant had seen the storm coming, and he was preparing to stand in the breach.

Chapter 8

The Sunset of the Just

"Faith and love are perceived through suffering."

The Final Burden

By the early 1990s, the body that had endured the harsh winters of the hen-house, the assaults of the Soviet mob, and the rigors of ascetic fasting began to fail. Father Gabriel had long prayed for a cross that would consume him for the sake of his people, and in his final years, that prayer was answered with a significant physical toll. He was diagnosed with edema, a condition historically referred to as dropsy, which caused painful swelling and fluid retention. Yet, even as his body began to falter, his spirit remained a fortress of defiance against comfort.

A turning point in his physical mobility came with a dramatic accident that carried spiritual significance. One evening, on the eve of the Feast of the Holy Trinity, Father Gabriel held a candle and announced to the nuns, "We have to keep vigil all night." He then moved toward the basement door, stating, "I'll go down and will not ascend." This proved to be a prophetic utterance. As he stepped onto the stairs, three steps collapsed beneath him, causing him to fall through and sustain serious injuries.

The nuns, alarmed, rushed to his side. Nun Nino and novice Melanie descended to find the Elder lying motionless on a trestle bed. "I thought he was dying," Nino recalled. "I was asking God to save our Elder." But Father Gabriel, even in agony, remained the master of the situation. He opened his eyes and ordered sternly, "Cover me with my mantle and go upstairs... Leave me now, I am a monk."

He had fractured his leg, an injury that was catastrophic for a man of his age and condition. For the last year and a half of his life, the "Flying Monk," who had once run through the streets of Tbilisi, was confined to his bed and could no longer walk. Nevertheless, he refused to allow this confinement to hinder his ministry. When the pain became unbearable, he would occasionally request assistance to be carried outside to sit in front of his cell, declaring, "Your life is my life. If you don't sacrifice yourself for people, nothing will be accomplished."

The War with the Demons

Even while confined to his bed, the spiritual warfare surrounding him intensified. The demons he had battled since the age of twelve did not grant him peace in his infirmity.

One day, after the Divine Liturgy, Father Gabriel collapsed at the threshold of the temple, striking his head once again. The nuns, unable to lift him onto the bed, moved him to his cell and placed him on the floor. He groaned in pain. In the ensuing confusion, one of the nuns stumbled and inadvertently struck the keys of an old grand piano that resided in his cell.

At the sound of the discordant notes, the bedridden Elder

suddenly sprang to his feet. To the astonishment of the sisters, he stood completely composed. "Play *Shalakho!*" he commanded, referring to a lively Georgian folk dance. He threw up his hands and began to dance, simultaneously singing and weeping.

"What happened to me?" he cried out, revealing the invisible struggle he faced. "I have been defeated by the devil. Yesterday he was bombarding the piano with stones. I ordered him to vanish, he responded that he will make me dance on that piano and he did." This moment provided a chilling insight into the reality he lived in—a world where the physical and spiritual realms were violently intertwined.

The Theology of the End

In the final year of his life, the tone of Father Gabriel's preaching underwent a significant transformation. For decades, he had focused on themes of repentance, love, and the fundamental need for God. However, as his own end drew near, he began to speak with urgency about the End of the World.

He cautioned his visitors that they were living in the times of the Antichrist. "You will witness his reign," he told them plainly. "He is at the door; he is not just knocking, he is breaking in."

His teachings regarding the End Times were specific and devoid of the vague symbolism often present in theological writings. He spoke of the "Seal of the Antichrist"—the number 666—not only as a spiritual concept but as a physical reality that would be imposed upon humanity. "Satan has set 666 traps," he warned. He prophesied that the seal would be visibly placed on the forehead and arms, likely beneath the skin using technology. "First, the seal will be offered to volunteers," he explained. "However, with the enthronement of the Antichrist, everyone will be pressed to accept the seal. Disobedience will be claimed as treachery."

He issued a stark warning about the forthcoming deception, particularly concerning "extraterrestrial" life. "During the antichrist times, the strongest temptation will be anticipation of salvation from cosmos, from 'humanoids,' 'extraterrestrials' that are actually masks of demons," he said. He urged the faithful not to look to the heavens for signs, as the demons would employ celestial phenomena to mislead the elect.

However, his message was not one of despair. He provided a survival strategy reminiscent of the Exodus. "You should flee to the mountains," he advised. "Do not fear! Just as the Israelites lacked nothing during their journey through the desert... similarly, God will care for those who seek freedom in Christ by fleeing to the mountains."

He assured them that nature itself would sustain the faithful. "One leaf of a plant will provide enough food for a month," he promised. "By making the sign of the cross, a lump of earth will be changed into bread." His message was unequivocal: those who rejected the seal and maintained their love for Christ would be safeguarded by the Holy Spirit, even if they had to live in the wilderness.

The Doctor and the Blood

As his edema worsened, a surgeon named Zurab Varazashvili was brought to Samtavro to attend to the Elder. Father Gabriel was a challenging patient; he often refused treatment, saying, "The first healer is God; next is a doctor." However, regarding one specific procedure, an unusual series of events unfolded that would only be understood years later.

Several days before his passing, the doctor determined that he needed to take a blood sample for testing. Initially, Father

Gabriel refused. The doctor, frustrated and desperate to assist, informed the monk that God would punish him if he did not permit the doctor to fulfill his duties. Reluctantly, Father Gabriel acquiesced.

The doctor drew 10 milliliters of blood into a test tube. A colleague then transported the sample toward Tbilisi for analysis. En route, the test tube slipped, fell, and the cork dislodged. Most of the blood spilled out, leaving only 2 milliliters. The colleague, disheartened, took what remained to the laboratory. The technicians assured him that it was sufficient. The tests revealed that surgery was necessary, but Father Gabriel categorically refused the procedure.

The 2 milliliters of blood were forgotten.

Years later, the doctor's colleague contacted him with astonishing news. During a laboratory renovation, he had discovered an old test tube that had been misplaced for four years. Upon examining it, they were astonished to find that the blood inside was fresh—neither coagulated, dried, nor decomposed. It appeared as though it had been drawn that very morning.

Dr. Zurab could hardly believe his eyes. He hurried to the laboratory, where they took a drop, prepared a smear, and examined it under a microscope. The blood cells were intact, a finding that defied scientific explanation.

They subsequently brought the blood sample to Patriarch Ilia II. Recognizing the sanctity of this relic, the Patriarch advised them to inter it in the earth where Father Gabriel had been laid to rest. For a time, the test tube remained buried in his grave, but it was eventually unearthed. Today, that incorrupt blood is preserved by Nun Paraskeva, who uses it to anoint the thousands of pilgrims who seek healing from the saint. It stands as a final, hidden miracle—a testament to the enduring life that transcends death itself.

The Crown of Thorns

Two weeks before his repose, a visitor presented Father Gabriel with a gift—an icon of the Holy Face of Christ, depicted wearing the crown of thorns.

Nun Paraskeva, hoping for a sign of recovery, said to the Elder, "Father Gabriel, you will be cured by the icon." She reminded him that an earlier icon of the Virgin Mary had previously provided him with relief.

Father Gabriel gazed at the image of the suffering Christ and shook his head. "Should it not be the crown of thorns, I would have been healed," he remarked, interpreting the spiritual semiotics of the gift. "It means I'll be dying in torments."

His prediction proved accurate. The pain he endured in his final days was excruciating. He spent nights in agony, struggling to breathe, his body swollen and frail. Yet, he never uttered a complaint. Instead, he devoted his remaining strength to preaching the only message that truly mattered.

"Remember, God is love," he told the stream of visitors who came to say goodbye. "Do as much kindness as you can... Be modest, for God showers His mercy upon His humble servants. Repent for your sins and do not delay for 'tomorrow,' as this delay is a snare set by the Devil."

The Departure

On the day before his death, Father Gabriel made his final announcement. "The time has come for my departure," he said.

He reached up with his right hand and gently caressed the icon of the Savior that hung above his bed. After a moment of silence, he communed with the God he had served since childhood. He then addressed the icon: "I have followed you, Christ, since the age of twelve. I am prepared; take me!"

The night became a vigil of suffering. He endured excruciating pain until 4:00 AM, when his breathing changed and became heavy and labored. In his delirium, or perhaps in a final vision of the unseen world, he began to call out: "Mother, mother; Sister, sister!"

The cell soon filled with people. The nuns from the convent, his biological family (including his mother, now Nun Anna), his doctor, and the priests gathered around his bed. Bishop Daniel arrived to recite the prayers for the dying.

Father Gabriel did not acknowledge them. His gaze remained fixed on the icon of St. Nicholas of Myra, which he regarded with profound love, as if the saint were present in the room to guide him.

As Bishop Daniel concluded the prayers for the departure of the soul, a change came over the Elder's face. The pain dissipated, replaced by a smile—the loving, mischievous, holy smile that had disarmed communists and comforted sinners.

He breathed his last on November 2, 1995. The Fool for Christ, the Confessor, the Monk Gabriel, had departed to be with the Lord.

The Burial and the Moving Earth

Father Gabriel had left explicit instructions for his burial. He did not want a coffin; he wished to be buried as a simple monk of old, wrapped only in a mat or sackcloth. "Dust I was, and to dust I have returned," he had written in his Last Will and Testament.

His body was laid out in the Church of the Transfiguration at Samtavro. For several days, the faithful came to pay their respects. Eventually, the time for interment arrived, and he was wrapped in a coarse mat.

When his body was laid to rest in the grave—a location

where St. Nino, the Enlightener of Georgia, had once toiled—a palpable hesitation enveloped the crowd. The depth of their affection for him rendered them unable to be the first shovel of dirt onto his remains; it felt akin to an act of violence against a beloved father.

Instead, they gently scattered earth around the edges of the grave, trying to fill it without covering him entirely.

Then, a final extraordinary event transpired. The earth began to shift. Witnesses reported that the soil, which had been loosely placed on the sides, seemed to flow autonomously. It moved "as if covering him, put him to the bosom," embracing him tenderly until his body was completely enveloped by the ground. The earth he had walked upon barefoot in the snow and upon which he had knelt upon in prayer now welcomed him home.

The Tomb of Miracles

A simple wooden cross was erected at his grave. The epitaph, as dictated by Gabriel himself, read: **"Truth is in the immortality of the spirit."**

Almost immediately, the grave became a source of profound power. The prophecy he had made during his lifetime—"Half of Georgia will come to my grave"—began to materialize. Individuals took oil from the lampada burning above his body and experienced healing from ailments such as cancer, blindness, and despair.

One woman, afflicted with tumors, received a vision of Father Gabriel smiling at her and was miraculously healed without the need for surgery. A prisoner suffering from a ruptured eardrum anointed himself with oil from the grave and regained his hearing.

However, perhaps the most remarkable miracle was the

continuation of his ministry of love. Even in death, he remained the "Mama Gabrieli" for the people. As he had promised, "I will not leave you. I will answer your prayers."

The monk who had feigned madness to conceal his holiness could no longer remain hidden. Although the sun had set on his earthly existence, the "radiant pillar of the end times" had just begun to shine.

Postscript: The Uncovering

Seventeen years later, in an unusually swift act of canonization, the Holy Synod of the Georgian Orthodox Church glorified him as a saint on December 20, 2012. On February 22, 2014, his relics were uncovered, revealing that his body was found to be incorrupt.

When his relics were transferred to the Svetitskhoveli Cathedral, the streets of Mtskheta and Tbilisi were overwhelmed. Hundreds of thousands of people lined the roads. The military was called in, not to arrest him this time, but to manage the vast crowd singing and weeping for their beloved Fool. The prophecy was fulfilled: the whole of Georgia had come to him.

Chapter 9

The Ever-Living Elder

"A monk, like a roaring lion, must uphold the Orthodox faith."

The Promise of Presence

When the earth embraced the body of Father Gabriel on November 2, 1995, many believed that the physical ministry of the "Great Love of the Twentieth Century" had concluded. They were mistaken. The Elder made a specific promise before his departure: "I will not leave you. I will answer your prayers." To his spiritual children, he reassured them, "Christ raised Lazarus from the dead; do you think it will be difficult for Him to raise me also? You will not be able to see me, but ask God in your prayers, and I'll always be with you."

What followed his repose was not silence but an outpouring of grace. The prophecy he uttered during his life-time—"Half of Georgia will come to my grave"—began to materialize with remarkable literalness. But it was not limited to Georgia. From the prison cells of the Ksanskaya Colony to the suburbs of Moscow, and from the sickbeds of Tbilisi to the streets of Paris, the "Fool for Christ" demonstrated that his power transcended the laws of mortality.

The School of the Spirit: Homilies of the Heart

Father Gabriel left no written theological treatises. He authored no books, founded no academic institutions, and held no high ecclesiastical office. His theology was inscribed directly onto the hearts of the faithful through short, piercing homilies that combined the simplicity of the Desert Fathers with the urgency of a prophet. As the faithful collected his sayings after his death, a cohesive and profound spiritual worldview emerged.

His central thesis was always love, but it was a love that demanded sacrifice. He famously wore a placard around his neck that read, "A man without love is like a pitcher without a bottom. No grace accumulates in him." He taught that love was not merely an emotion but a learned skill requiring effort. "Whoever learns to love will be happy," he said. "Only do not think that love is an inborn talent. One can learn love, and we must." He warned that "God will not accept empty words. God loves deeds. Good deeds are what love is."

He was particularly stern regarding the sin of judgment, which he viewed as the destroyer of love. He used vivid agricultural imagery to illustrate the danger of pride: "Never judge; the only Judge is God. Who condemns resembles an empty ear of wheat, whose head is always uplifted." He reminded his listeners that the "bridles" of sinners are often loosened by God for reasons unknown to us. "If you see a killer, a whore, or a drunkard prostrated on the ground, never judge them, since their bridles have been loosened by God while yours are held firm," he taught. "If God sets free your rein, you will find yourself in a worse condition, commit the sin which you had condemned, and get ruined."

The Physician of the Hopeless

If his words served as medicine for the soul, his intercessions became the remedy for the body. Following his burial, the oil from the lampada burning at his grave in Samtavro became a conduit for miraculous healings that confounded the medical community.

The accounts were recorded with clinical precision by the monastery and the faithful. Lela Tsirekidze, a resident of Tbilisi, was diagnosed with tumors on her breast and internal organs. The oncologists insisted on immediate surgery, giving her only two weeks to live without it. Desperate, Lela visited Father Gabriel's grave. There, she experienced a vision: "Fr. Gabriel was standing there and smiling at me." Filled with a sudden, inexplicable faith, she declined the operation and began anointing herself with oil from the grave. Two months later, an examination revealed that "nothing resembling a tumor was found in my system."

Another woman, Pelagea Tamarashvili from the village of Saguramo, suffered from fibroma and myoma. She attempted to anoint herself with the elder's oil twice but felt relief followed by a relapse. Discouraged, she stopped, telling herself, "It doesn't help." That night, she had a dream. A priest with a large beard appeared and gently admonished her: "Here you are lamenting, 'It doesn't help, it doesn't help'—but what can help you if you haven't prayed? Pray, and you will see whether it helps or not... You say that you believe, but you don't pray—

what kind of faith is that?" Upon waking, Pelagea resumed the anointing, this time with prayer. A subsequent ultrasound revealed she was completely healed, leaving her doctor in shock.

The miracles extended to the most agonizing conditions. Makvala Davitashvili, suffering from severe psoriasis that covered her entire body with sores, found her skin cleared after just four anointings. Suliko Gvinjilia, afflicted with severe cirrhosis of the liver, anointed herself and sought the Elder's blessing to be admitted to the hospital. Not only was she admitted, but the ultrasound revealed that the cirrhosis had vanished.

The Prisoner's Hope

Perhaps the most touching were the letters that began to arrive at Samtavro from the prisons of Georgia. The "prisoner #666," who once languished in a KGB isolation cell, became a special patron of the incarcerated.

In the Ksanskaya Colony, a church dedicated to St. Nicholas was built, and a prisoner named Vasiliy Narindoshvili started a ministry of applying Father Gabriel's oil to his fellow inmates. The results were astonishing. Vasiliy himself had suffered a ruptured eardrum from beatings in 1994-1995, with blood and pus constantly draining from his ear. After two anointings, the pain ceased, and 80-90% of his hearing returned.

Miracles within the prison continued to multiply. A ten-month-old baby, brought to visit a prisoner, fell gravely ill with a high fever. The doctors were helpless. The prisoners sent for the oil. When Vasiliy arrived, the weakened baby reached out to him. Vasiliy anointed the child's forehead and placed a drop on his pinky finger, which the baby licked. The child fell asleep and woke up completely healthy.

Another prisoner, Guram Managadze, suffering from severe stomach ulcers, was healed instantly after his cellmates recited the "Our Father" and administered the oil to him. Artur Soukasyan, whose foot was festering and rotting, was anointed and had earth from the Elder's grave sprinkled on his wound; the next morning, his foot was healthy.

The Jacket and the Icon

Physical objects associated with the saint also became vessels of grace. In the Monastery of the Nativity of the Most Holy Mother of God, a unique relic was preserved: Father Gabriel's jacket, worn beneath his monastic mantle. Pilgrims discovered that the jacket was accessible to them. They would wear it, feeling a tangible weight of holiness. From the pocket hung a small silver cross. One pilgrim described the experience of wearing the jacket while reading morning prayers as a time when "a great number of unbelievable things happened," attesting to the palpable presence of the saint in his personal belongings.

In Moscow, the veneration of the Georgian Elder took a miraculous turn involving a book. Maria Pukhova, an editor at a publishing house, was working on a book titled *Elder Gabriel: A Heart Full of Love*. Before she began, Father Gabriel appeared to her in a dream. She found herself in a grand church with Catholicos-Patriarchs in golden vestments. Father Gabriel approached her, smiling and wearing golden robes with a shining cross. He placed his arm around her shoulder and said, "I've been looking for you! I've found you!"

This spiritual connection manifested physically on August 24, 2018. Two days before Maria was to travel to Georgia, the cover of the book in her home began to stream myrrh. Small "glowing" spots of oil appeared on the image of the Elder. On his birthday, August 26, as parishioners gathered to read the Akathist hymn, the myrrh intensified, forming large drops and oil stains that allowed the faithful to anoint themselves. This phenomenon was not isolated to her copy; other parishioners reported their copies of the book streaming myrrh as well.

The Triumph of the Humble

The swell of popular veneration could not be overlooked. On December 20, 2012, only seventeen years after his repose— an exceptionally brief period in the traditions of the Church— the Holy Synod of the Georgian Orthodox Church officially canonized Archimandrite Gabriel as a saint. He was bestowed the title "Saint Gabriel, Confessor and Fool for Christ."

The canonization ignited a national celebration, but the true climax occurred on February 22, 2014, when his holy relics were uncovered. The grave at Samtavro, which had been a quiet place of pilgrimage, became the focal point of the nation. The government and the Church anticipated crowds, but they were unprepared for the overwhelming influx of humanity that descended upon Mtskheta.

Hundreds of thousands of people lined the streets. The military had to be deployed to manage the crowds, but unlike the soldiers of 1965 who had guarded the burning portrait of Lenin, these soldiers were there to honor the man who had burned it. The relics were transferred to Svetitskhoveli Cathedral and then to the Holy Trinity Cathedral in Tbilisi, paralyzing the capital with a procession of love.

Father Gabriel's body was found to be incorrupt. He was placed in a glass reliquary, adorned in the vestments of a priest and the simple diadem he wore in life. His prophecy had been fulfilled: he had endured the fire of persecution, endured the ice of rejection, and now he belongs to the ages.

The Eternal Diadem

Today, the relics of Saint Gabriel rest in the Samtavro Transfiguration Church, enshrined in a special crypt. However, his true resting place is in the homes and hearts of the faithful. His image—often depicting him with a warm, knowing smile and a diadem fashioned from scrap metal—can be found in cars, schools, and homes across Georgia and Russia.

He remains a "radiant pillar of the end of times," a guide for those navigating the complexities of the modern world. His message, stripped of all pretense, remains as simple and profound as the Gospel itself: "Truth is in the immortality of the spirit."

The boy who built churches from matchboxes, the youth who collected bones from the mud, the monk who burned the idol of the age, and the fool who feigned drunkenness to hide his tears had finally completed his work. He had shown the world that true power does not reside in the state, wealth, or the praise of men. It lies in the "foolishness" of the Cross, in the unstoppable, bottomless pitcher of love that pours forth grace upon a thirsty world.

As he promised, he has not left. He is waiting at Samtavro.

Chapter 10

The School of the Spirit

"The last time a man will be saved is by love, humbleness, and kindness. Kindness will open the gates of Heaven; humbleness will lead into Heaven; the man whose heart is filled with love will see God."

The Pedagogy of the Unexpected

While the major events of Father Gabriel's life—the burning of the Lenin portrait, the years of persecution, and the final repose—form the skeleton of his hagiography, the true flesh and blood of his ministry is found in the daily, often bizarre, interactions he had with the nuns and pilgrims at Samtavro. He did not run a conventional parish. He operated a school of the spirit where the curriculum was unpredictable, the exams were sudden, and the grading system was based entirely on humility.

He did not write books, yet he wrote upon the human heart with a precision that was often terrifying. As Nun Paraskeva, his faithful cell attendant, observed, "Father Gabriel's thoughts were constantly with God." Yet, this constant communion did not make him distant; it made him hyper-aware of the spiritual state of everyone around him. He used every tool at his disposal —humor, shock, feigned anger, and prophetic insight—to chip away the hardened calcification of pride from the souls entrusted to him.

The Lesson of the Eggs

Father Gabriel's teachings on obedience were not delivered in dry lectures but in living parables that often carried a sting for the disobedient. He taught that obedience was not merely a monastic rule but a spiritual law of the universe, the violation of which brought immediate rot.

One day, a group of laymen came to visit the Elder, bringing with them a gift of thirty eggs. In the time of post-Soviet shortages, such a gift was precious. Father Gabriel looked at the offering and gave a specific, seemingly arbitrary instruction. "Leave fifteen," he blessed them, "and take back the rest."

The visitors, perhaps thinking they were being more generous than the monk, or perhaps thinking his request was just another eccentricity, refused to take the eggs back. They insisted on leaving all thirty, believing they were doing a good deed. Father Gabriel did not argue. He let them leave the full gift.

However, the laws of spiritual physics, as Father Gabriel understood them, could not be mocked. A few days later, when the nuns went to use the eggs, they discovered a strange phenomenon. Exactly fifteen of the eggs were fresh and usable. The other fifteen—the "fruit of disobedience"—had gone rotten. As the Elder later explained using a story from the desert fathers about cabbage planted upside down, "You see, my son, this is the fruit of obedience."

The Doctor and the Sheep

Even gratitude was a complex subject in Father Gabriel's court. He demanded that labor be rewarded, and he refused to let spiritual debts go unpaid. When his health began to fail, a surgeon named Zurab Varazashvili attended to him. Father Gabriel, who often refused medical help saying, "The first healer is God, next is a doctor," eventually allowed the treatment.

To express his gratitude, the Elder decided to give the doctor a sheep that had been sacrificed to the Convent. He presented the animal to the surgeon with a spiritual maxim: "The workers deserve a reward. To bestow gratitude to a doctor means to glorify God."

But the doctor, perhaps out of modesty or a secular sense of professional ethics, refused the gift. He insisted that his assistance should be gratuitous. He would not take the sheep.

The result was immediate and baffling to the rational mind. The very same day the doctor refused the gift, the sheep died. Father Gabriel was not pleased with this display of false modesty. He rebuked the doctor, revealing the spiritual mechanics behind the event: "Nobody has ever heard of the sacrificed animals dying at the Convent; this is the first time because of your disobedience, my neighbor." The Elder then offered him another sheep. This time, the doctor, having learned that refusing a saint is more dangerous than accepting a fee, accepted it with thanks.

The Chanticleer

For the nuns of Samtavro, life with Father Gabriel was a trial by fire. He had a unique ability to target the specific insecurities or vanities of a novice and press on them until they broke, revealing the humble spirit underneath.

When Nun Nana (Kutateladze) first arrived at the convent on September 11, the feast of the Beheading of St. John the Forerunner, she was introduced to Father Gabriel in the refectory. She was the niece of the Abbess, Heghumene Ketevan, and perhaps there was a danger of nepotism or pride in her heart. Father Gabriel looked at her, pondering for a moment. He did not offer a pious welcome.

"Who, this chanticleer, this chanticleer?" he began to say, using a word that compared her to a noisy rooster. He repeated the taunt over and over, "this chanticleer," until the young woman, mortified and overwhelmed, ran out of the refectory weeping bitterly.

It seemed cruel, but it was a test. He was checking to see if she would stay despite the insult. Later, when Nana tried to slip away from the convent without his blessing to visit her parents, thinking she had escaped his notice, she found him waiting for her upon her return. She expected him to shout. Instead, he patted her shoulder, his eyes filled with tears. "My child," he said, revealing the depth of his love, "you know everyone loves you, and should you not return, I would have left the monastery as well." He had been praying for her return the entire time she was gone. The "Chanticleer" had been humbled, but she was also deeply loved.

The Snake and the Science

Father Gabriel often went to great lengths to hide his miracle-working abilities behind the mask of natural causes or medical science. He did not want to be worshipped as a healer.

One day, Nun Nino was bitten by a snake in the courtyard of the convent. The bite was serious; there were two deep wounds on her leg. Terrified, the nuns ran to Father Gabriel. The Elder acted quickly. He applied oil and sprinkled holy water on the wounds. To the amazement of the sisters, the wounds were cured immediately. The poison was neutralized by his prayer.

But Father Gabriel could not let the moment stand as a naked miracle. He immediately switched into his stern persona. "Now, go quickly to a doctor!" he ordered strictly.

It was a time of crisis in Georgia—famine, no electricity, and scarce medicine. The doctors at the hospital helplessly shrugged their shoulders, awaiting a pitiful outcome for a snakebite victim in such conditions. But the nun recovered completely. While the doctors were puzzled, Father Gabriel was in his cell, commending "his fervent thanksgiving prayers to God." He had used the doctor as a cover story for the grace of God.

The Theology of the Theater

Father Gabriel's approach to the world outside Orthodoxy was complex. He was a strict dogmatist who called ecumenism a "super heresy," yet his heart was open to every human being. He demonstrated that one could hold to the truth without hating those outside of it.

He recounted a story of visiting a synagogue. To the shock of the congregation, he ascended the place from where the Bible was read and "started preaching of Christ." The people were confused and called the Magister. But instead of throwing the monk out, the Magister listened. He invited the Elder to his office, where they had "long talks about Christ." Father Gabriel respected their veneration of the Prophet Moses, whom he also worshipped venerably, and found a way to speak to them of the Messiah.

His visit to a mosque was equally disarming. When he entered, the people were having tea. Seeing an Orthodox monk in a mantle, they rose to their feet—a sign of respect that transcended religious boundaries—and asked him to join them. "We were talking about love and parted with love," Father Gabriel recalled simply.

However, his reception was not always warm. When he visited a Baptist church, his appearance caused irritation. They called their supervisor, and Father Gabriel was kicked out. Even in rejection, he was testing the spirits, seeking those who would respond to love.

His love for the dramatic extended to the secular arts as well. He loved the popular Georgian opera *Daisi*. He would often go to the Opera House to see it. There was a scene where a character representing the Catholicos (Patriarch) blesses the people. Whenever this scene occurred, Father Gabriel would rise to his feet in the theater and bow down low. He knew the man on stage was an actor, but he honored the image of the dignity he represented. On one occasion, there was confusion on stage during an intermission. Taking advantage of the chaos, Father Gabriel "climbed the stage preaching about Christ," turning a secular performance into a pulpit.

The "Eighth Ecumenical Council"

As his health declined, his humor and prophetic insight seemed to sharpen. In 1995, the Georgian Church Council was convened at the Svetitskhoveli Cathedral. It was a local council, a gathering of bishops to discuss church matters.

Father Gabriel, watching from his tower in Samtavro, called out to Nun Nino (Julakidze). He pointed a trembling finger toward the great cathedral and made a grand, ironic proclamation. "Do you know," he said, "the Eighth Ecumenical Council is being held there now!"

The nun smiled, thinking it was a joke. The Seven Ecumenical Councils are the pillars of Orthodoxy, and no council since the 8th century holds that title. Father Gabriel saw her smile and asked her why. Then, with the fierce pride of a confessor who loved his nation's spiritual heritage, he added: "Is there anywhere Orthodox except Georgia?!"

It was a statement of spiritual geography. For Gabriel, Georgia was not just a country; it was the lot of the Mother of God, the last bastion, the spiritual "Athos" from which he refused to depart.

The Volts of the Spirit

The physical toll of bearing such grace was immense. Nun Paraskeva witnessed moments where the Elder seemed to act as a conduit for energies that the human body is not designed to handle.

One day, she heard his weak voice calling her. She ran back to find him in convulsions. It looked as if "strong electric current was passing through his body". He was shaking, vibrating with an invisible power. After a while, his power of speech returned, but the Voice that came out of him was not his own. It was a Voice prophesying Georgia's fate. Nun Paraskeva tried to memorize the words, but they were erased from her memory, perhaps intended only for the spirit and not for the historical record.

When they raised him to his feet, she asked him what had

happened. "500 volts was nothing compared with the energy possessed by God," he answered.

He spoke of the Holy Spirit not as an abstract concept but as a visible reality. When asked if the descent of the Holy Spirit is visible, he gave a precise, almost technical description: "It looks like two small circles appearing in the form of fireflies, making circular rotations that gradually grow bigger and brighter. At this moment, the Holy Spirit is descending on you... You have a feeling you possess the universe; you are able to see everything that is going on around you; even if the whole army or the whole world is raised against you, you will over-power them without any effort."

He also shared a vision of the feast of Pentecost. Paraskeva had dreamed of a white dove as big as an eagle descending. When she told Father Gabriel, he confirmed it. "It's interesting to note that the white dove abides in the Convent," the source notes, linking the spiritual vision to the physical reality of the monastery.

The Last Warning

As the end of his earthly life approached, Father Gabriel's warnings about the "Last Days" became more frequent, but they were always tempered with the promise of divine protection for the faithful. He spoke of the "seal" of the Antichrist, warning that it would be placed on the forefinger, not the palm, and would be "put under the skin with the help of the computer."

Yet, he offered a loophole of grace for those coerced: "If someone had the Antichrist seal impression made by force, in God's sight the person will be considered as a virgin disgraced against her will. The seal won't have any effect if made against one's will."

He assured his flock that nature itself would sustain them. "One leaf of a plant will provide enough food for a month. By making the sign of the cross, a lump of earth will be changed into bread."

The Final Act

Even in his dying days, Father Gabriel remained a "Fool" for Christ, using his behavior to hide his holiness. When he fell down at the threshold of the temple and hit his head, he was dragged to his cell in agony. Yet, when a nun accidentally hit the keys of the piano in his cell, he sprang up and danced the *Shalakho*, claiming the devil made him do it. It was a performance to distract them from his suffering and his sanctity.

He prepared his spiritual children for his departure with a promise that defied death. "I am leaving you this testament: Raise your prayers for everyone; your prayers will move the mountains. Love each other."

When asked what they would do without him, he replied with the confidence of a man who knew exactly where he was going: "Christ raised Lazarus from the dead; do you think it will be difficult for Him to raise me also? You will not be able to see me, but ask God in your prayers, and I'll always be with you."

And so, the Monk Gabriel, the Confessor, the Fool, the Teacher, prepared to leave his cell in the King Mirian Tower for a cell in the Kingdom of Heaven. He had fought the beast, he had collected the bones of martyrs, he had built a church from trash, and he had taught a generation of Georgians that the only path to survival was love.

"Truth," he dictated for his epitaph, "is in the immortality of the spirit." His spirit, indeed, was just beginning its greatest work.

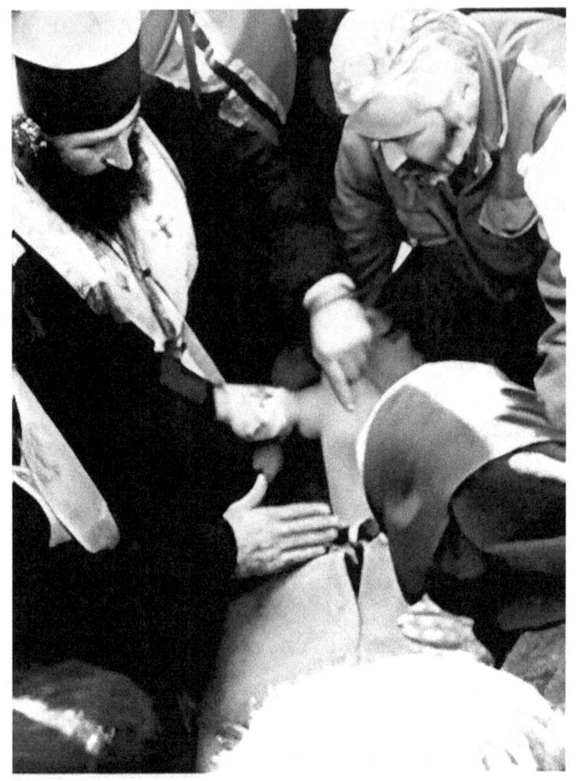

Chapter 11

The Tower of the Spirit

"For the Lord, it is not so important whether you are a monk or a layman; what is important is to have a thirst for God. Through this thirst, a man can be saved. The monk will be judged by monastic canons, while the secular will be judged by worldly rules."

By the early 1990s, the round tower of King Mirian at Samtavro Convent had become the epicenter of a spiritual earthquake that was quietly shaking Georgia. To the uninitiated, the cell within looked like the hoard of an eccentric collector; to the faithful, it was a portal to the Kingdom of Heaven. The brick walls were almost completely covered with icons of various sizes, shapes, and styles—some paper, some painted, many rescued from the dumps of the atheistic era.

But amidst this gallery of saints, Father Gabriel kept a stark reminder of earthly futility: a human skull. He would point to it, the head of an unknown ascetic, and tell his visitors that a monk "simply must have such a thing" to keep his mind fixed on the fleeting nature of mortality.

Life inside this tower was governed not by the clock, but by the unpredictable rhythms of the Holy Spirit. Father Gabriel did not just pray; he engaged in a combat that was often visible to those around him. His cell attendant, Nun Paraskeva, once witnessed a terrifying physical manifestation of this spiritual energy. She heard his weak voice calling her and ran back to find him in convulsions. It looked as if a "strong electric current was passing through his body." When they managed to raise him to his feet, he explained the sensation with a comparison from the physical world: "500 volts was nothing compared with the energy possessed by God."

He described the descent of the Holy Spirit with the precision of a technician. He told a cleric that it "looks like two small circles appearing in the form of fireflies, making circular rotations that gradually grow bigger and brighter." At that moment, he explained, "You have a feeling you possess the universe... even if the whole army or the whole world is raised against you, you will overpower them without any effort."

The School of the Mothers

Father Gabriel knew that he was not just saving souls in the present; he was preparing the future leadership of the Georgian Church. His methods for training the future abbesses were rigorous, prophetic, and often humiliating.

He had a special relationship with Mother Ketevan (Kopaliani), whom he prophesied would become the "Mother of Georgia" long before she was tonsured.

When she was appointed Heghumene (Abbess), the burden was immense, and the nuns were often disobedient. Once, in a moment of despair, she came to him complaining,

"Father Gabriel, I can't stand it anymore. I have to remove my Cross."

The Elder did not offer tea and sympathy. He cast a distressed look at her, turned toward his icons with raised hands, and then delivered a stern rebuke: "Be patient, my Sister and Mother, don't remove your Cross; the one who does it will take responsibility for it... You will be thrown by God into a burning furnace to be tested and purified."

He taught her that the dignity of her office was not a title of honor but a mechanism for the "mortification of self-esteem and pride."

With another spiritual daughter, Ketevan Tochilashvili (later Mother Ketevan), his method was equally disarming. The first time she visited his cell, sent by Mother Paraskeva, the Elder lay on his couch with a broken leg. He looked at her and shouted joyfully, "Oh! What a guest I have today!" He then immediately began to weep, telling her that her life would be very hard, foreseeing the sorrows she would endure. But then, the mood shifted instantly.

"Help me get up and give me my *kukul-bartukul*," he commanded. The young woman had no idea what a *kukul-bartukul* was. Mother Paraskeva reached out to help, but the Elder stopped her sternly. He forced the newcomer to assist him, then sat her down and appointed her the "Tamada" (toastmaster) of the meal. For five or six hours, he spoke only to her, ignoring everyone else in the room, teaching her that the most important thing for a monk is "unconditional obedience."

The Economics of Providence

Father Gabriel's relationship with money was non-existent. He treated currency as a tool for testing the hearts of others. He would sometimes hire a taxi and leave without paying to test the driver's patience, or conversely, he would overpay drastically to confuse them.

One day, he was preparing to go to Tbilisi to purchase essential articles for the Convent. He had exactly one hundred rubles—a significant sum at the time. While waiting at the bus stop, he overheard two beekeepers lamenting their misfortune. They were in desperate need of exactly one hundred rubles to save their bees and sustain their livelihood. Without a moment's hesitation, Father Gabriel took the money from his pocket, gave it to the strangers, and returned to the Convent empty-handed.

The laws of spiritual economics, however, are swift. The very next day, two well-known artists visited the Elder. Moved by his holiness, they donated one thousand rubles to him. Father Gabriel smiled at the witnesses and articulated the formula: "Whatever is given out for kind deeds is rewarded ten times by God."

He was not afraid to beg, not for his own need, but to humble the proud. He once took a novice, Theodora, to the Church of the Holy Trinity in Tbilisi. He stood there and began begging for alms. He made the novice stand next to him, sharing in the public humiliation. He collected the money, gave it all to the poor, and then gave whatever was left to the novice. He would say, "I am a worm, earth and dust," and through these acts, he forced those around him to shed their social pretensions.

The Vision of the End

As the political situation in Georgia disintegrated in the early 1990s, Father Gabriel's gaze turned increasingly toward the eschaton—the End Times. His warnings were specific, stripping away the abstract theology often associated with the Apocalypse.

He warned that the "antichrist is at the door; he is not just knocking; he is breaking in."

He spoke of the "seal" of the Antichrist (666) not merely as a symbol, but as a technological reality that would be placed "under the skin with the help of the computer." He was particularly emphatic about the deception that would come from the skies. "During the antichrist times," he warned, "the strongest temptation will be anticipation of salvation from cosmos, from 'humanoids,' 'extraterrestrials' that are actually masks of demons." He advised his spiritual children rarely to look up at the sky during those times, lest they be deceived by false signs.

Yet, he offered a prophecy of hope that linked the fate of his nation with the Holy Mountain of Athos. He predicted that the famous Iveron Icon of the Mother of God would leave Mount Athos. "Leaving of the Holy Mountain by the icon of the Iberian Holy Virgin will be followed by bell ringing, and churches will bow to commemorate the farewell," he said. He added a modern twist to this ancient expectation: "All this will be shown on TV, so that the whole world could see it and come to Georgia, who want to save their souls."

He insisted that Georgia was the "lot" of the Mother of God and would be protected. When the Abbot of Xeropotamou Monastery from Athos visited and lamented that the Virgin had "abandoned Georgia," Father Gabriel rebuked him so fiercely that the Athonite fell to his knees. "I am here, on my Athos," Gabriel told him. "I won't exchange my Georgia for Athos."

The French Dream and the Scissors

Father Gabriel's reach extended far beyond the borders of

Georgia, often invading the dreams of those who had never met him. A striking example involves Maia Chanturia, a Georgian woman living in France. Distressed by the temptations facing her son, also named Gabriel, she prayed for a saint of the same name to intercede.

She had a dream. She was in the Monastery of Odeli in Alsace. Standing before a shop window of icons, she saw a monk in a *kamelaukion* (monastic hat) with a large Crucifixion cross on his chest. It was Father Gabriel. In the dream, the Elder walked past her companions and approached a woman referred to as "Madame N." He stood behind this woman and said chillingly, "A foul odor from her is from the same sin."

Then, pointing in the direction of Georgia, he gave Maia a bizarre command: "Cut that dress into small pieces and distribute among those who need."

When Maia woke and told "Madame N" about the dream, the woman began to weep. She revealed that years earlier, she had visited Mtskheta. Father Gabriel had met her and asked her to sew him a dress (a cassock or garment), but she had refused. The dream was a piercing reminder of her lack of charity. Maia later sent a portrait she drew of the Elder to the convent, testifying that "Every Georgian living in France feels" his prayers.

The Myrrh and the Book

Decades after his repose, the physical objects associated with Father Gabriel continued to behave as if they were alive. In Moscow, Maria Pukhova was editing a book titled *Elder Gabriel: A Heart Full of Love*. She was struggling with the manuscript when the Elder appeared to her in a dream, smiling and saying, "I've been looking for you! I've found you!"

On August 24, 2018, just before Maria was to travel to

Georgia, the cover of this book in her home began to stream myrrh. Small "glowing" spots of oil appeared on the image of the Elder. On his birthday, August 26, as parishioners gathered to read the Akathist hymn, the myrrh intensified. "Larger drops and oil stains had appeared, so we could even anoint ourselves with it," Maria testified. This was not an isolated incident; other copies of the book in the homes of parishioners also began to exude the fragrant oil.

Similarly, in the Monastery of the Nativity of the Most Holy Mother of God, Father Gabriel's jacket—the one he wore under his mantle, with a small silver cross hanging from the pocket—became a source of pilgrimage. Visitors were allowed to put it on. One pilgrim, Nino, described wearing it while reading morning prayers and experiencing a "great number of unbelievable things," feeling the tangible weight of the saint's protection.

The Uncovering

Father Gabriel died on November 2, 1995. He had requested to be buried without a coffin, wrapped only in a mat, in the place where St. Nino had labored. "Dust I was, and to dust I have returned," he wrote in his Last Will and Testament.

For nineteen years, his grave at Samtavro was a place of quiet miracles. But on February 22, 2014, the prophecy that "Half of Georgia will come to my grave" was fulfilled with over-whelming literalness. The Holy Synod had canonized him in December 2012, an exceptionally short time after his death, citing his extraordinary confession of faith. Now, the time had come to uncover his relics.

The scenes in Mtskheta were biblical. The government and Church expected crowds, but they were unprepared for the ocean of humanity that flooded the ancient capital. The military had to be called in—not to persecute the monk as they had in 1965, but to manage the hundreds of thousands of people singing, weeping, and pressing forward to catch a glimpse of the "Fool."

When the earth was removed, his body was found to be incorrupt. He was lifted from the grave, still wrapped in his simple vestments, with the diadem of the "King of the Spirit" on his head. The relics were translated to the Svetitskhoveli Cathedral and then to the Holy Trinity Cathedral in Tbilisi. The traffic in the capital was paralyzed. People lined the highways, throwing flowers in the path of the hearse. The "madman" with the White Ticket, the "psychopath" #666, had conquered the nation not with a sword, but with love.

The Eternal Present

Today, Saint Gabriel rests in a glass shrine in the Samtavro Transfiguration Church. But as he promised, "I will not leave you." He continues to act with the same unpredictable, fierce, and tender love he showed in life.

He appears to prisoners in their cells, healing ruptured eardrums and stomach ulcers with oil from his lampada. He appears to women in hospitals, telling them to pray instead of complaining, healing tumors that doctors called incurable. He brings together those who love him, creating a spiritual family that spans continents.

In the end, his life was the ultimate subversion of the world's values. He wore a crown made of scrap metal to mock the crowns of worldly power. He feigned drunkenness to expose the intoxication of pride. He burned the image of a tyrant to reveal the image of God.

As he wrote in his final testament: "The purpose of life and of this whole visible world is the acquisition of the Kingdom of

God, drawing near to God and inheriting Eternal Life... Truth is in the immortality of the spirit."

The "Great Love of the Twentieth Century" had completed his course, but his ministry had only just begun. He waits at Samtavro, smiling his mischievous, holy smile, ready to welcome anyone brave enough to approach the fire.

Chapter 12

The Blood and the Oil

"Your soul dies when you do nothing to defend your faith; but when you die to defend your faith, the door to the Kingdom of Heaven opens before you."

The Surgeon's Dilemma

In the final weeks of Father Gabriel's earthly life, his body, which had served as a relentless instrument of asceticism, began to succumb to the frailty of human nature. He suffered from severe edema, a condition that caused painful swelling, and his stomach was failing him. The man who had walked barefoot through snow and slept in a drafty hen-house was now confined to a bed of pain.

To attend to the dying monk, the Patriarchate sent a distinguished physician, Dr. Zurab Georgievich Varazi (also referred to as Varazashvili), an excellent surgeon known for his skill. Father Gabriel, true to his "foolish" nature, was not an easy patient. He often refused treatment, proclaiming that "the first healer is God, next is a doctor," and insisting that he did not have the right to do whatever he wanted with his body without a blessing.

Several days before the Elder's repose, Dr. Zurab decided that a blood test was medically necessary to understand the extent of the organ failure. He approached Father Gabriel with the request. The Elder refused. He had prepared himself for death and saw little point in the invasive procedures of modern medicine. However, the doctor was persistent. He appealed to the monk's sense of obedience and responsibility, telling him that God would punish him, the doctor, if he failed to treat his patient properly because of the patient's obstinacy. Father Gabriel, who would never want to be the cause of another's spiritual stumbling, finally relented.

The doctor drew 10 milliliters of venous blood into a standard glass test tube. He corked it and handed it to a colleague who was to transport it immediately to the laboratory in Tbilisi for analysis.

What happened next seemed like a mundane accident, a clumsy mistake that would be forgotten in the rush of the Elder's final days. As the colleague was driving toward the capital, the test tube slipped from his hands. It fell inside the car, the cork popped loose, and the precious sample spilled. The driver frantically tried to salvage what he could, but most of the blood was lost. When he uprighted the tube, only 2 milliliters remained.

Distressed but pressing on, he delivered the meager sample to the laboratory. The technicians reassured him that 2 milliliters was sufficient for the required tests. The analysis was performed, revealing a dire picture: surgery was necessary. But Father Gabriel categorically refused the operation, and the next day, November 2, 1995, he departed to the Lord.

The test tube with the remaining 2 milliliters of blood was set aside. In the chaos of the funeral and the grief of the nation, it was forgotten.

The Resurrection of the Blood

Four years passed. The laboratory in Tbilisi was undergoing renovations. Drawers were emptied, shelves were cleared, and old samples were discarded. Amidst the clutter of medical history, the doctor's colleague stumbled upon an old test tube. It had been lost behind equipment, gathering dust for forty-eight months.

He picked it up, expecting to see a dried, black crust or a putrefied residue of decomposed biological matter. Instead, he froze. The blood inside the tube was liquid. It was bright red. It looked as if it had been drawn from a living vein that very morning.

Shocked and unable to believe his own eyes, he immediately called Dr. Zurab. The surgeon traveled to the laboratory, skepticism battling with amazement. When he saw the tube, he confirmed it was the sample taken from Father Gabriel. Scientifically, this was impossible. Blood coagulates, separates, and decomposes rapidly once removed from the body. To verify what they were seeing, the doctors took a syringe, drew a single drop, made a smear, and examined it under a microscope.

The pathology report was even more baffling than the visual inspection. The blood cells were intact. There was no hemolysis, no decomposition. The blood was "alive," maintaining the properties of a fresh sample despite four years of abandonment in a room with fluctuating temperatures.

The doctors, realizing they had stumbled upon a holy mystery, brought the blood to His Holiness, Catholicos-Patriarch Ilia II. They explained the impossibility of the phenomenon: "We took this blood four years ago, but it is as fresh as if it had been taken yesterday."

The Patriarch, perceiving the sanctity of the relic, advised them not to keep it in a lab or a museum, but to return it to the earth. "Give this blood over to the earth where Fr. Gabriel reposes," he instructed.

Obediently, they buried the test tube in the soil of Father Gabriel's grave at the Samtavro Monastery. For a time, it rested there, mingling its holiness with the earth that was already working miracles. However, the faithful were constantly unearthing the grave, taking soil home in bags and pockets to heal their sick. Fearing the test tube might be broken or lost in the fervor of the pilgrims, Mother Paraskeva, the Elder's faithful cell attendant who now tended his grave, retrieved it from the soil.

She became the guardian of the blood. Today, she keeps this biological impossibility—a liquid relic of the man who died decades ago—and uses it to bless the pilgrims. She does not anoint them with the blood itself, but holds the tube and makes the sign of the Cross over those who come seeking help. And the blood, which refused to die, continues to bring life.

The Exorcism at the Grave

The power of this relic was demonstrated with terrifying clarity one sunny day at Samtavro. The grave was crowded with pilgrims, as usual. A man approached, leading a teenage boy by the hand. The boy was somewhat chubby and visibly agitated, his behavior erratic. The father spoke to him softly, trying to persuade him to approach the holy ground.

They reached the marble tombstone. The father tried to gently force his son to kneel, a standard posture of reverence for pilgrims. But the boy suddenly locked his legs. He became obstinate, refusing to bend. He began to rock back and forth, shifting his weight from foot to foot in a rhythmic, agitated motion that grew faster and more abrupt by the second.

At that moment, Mother Paraskeva emerged from her tent. She saw the spiritual struggle manifesting as physical resistance. She did not hesitate. She retrieved the test tube containing the Elder's blood. With a quick, deft motion, she approached the boy and made the sign of the Cross over his head with the relic.

The reaction was instant and inhuman. The boy let out a loud, guttural noise that witnesses described as exactly like a "horse's neighing." He broke free from his father's grip and took to his heels. But he did not run like a boy; he galloped. He moved with the gait of a terrified animal, fleeing the presence of a holiness that the entity inside him could not bear.

The father chased after him. Fifteen minutes later, they returned, trying again. The scene repeated itself. Each time the blood was brought near, the boy was repelled by an invisible force, unable to withstand the proximity of the Confessor's living remains.

The Oil of Gladness

While the blood was a relic administered by the nun, the oil from the lampada that burned perpetually at Father Gabriel's grave became the medicine of the people. A large canopy protected the grave from the elements, covering a flowerbed sprinkled with dry, black earth. Amidst the flowers burned the lampada. Pilgrims would bring small bottles, and a young man or woman would carefully top them off with oil, wiping away spilled drops with reverence. This oil traveled to hospitals, homes, and prisons, carrying with it a track record of medical impossibilities.

The Death of Cancer

Lela Tsirekidze, a resident of Tbilisi, found herself facing a death sentence. In March, she was diagnosed with tumors on her breast and internal organs. The diagnosis was aggressive. The oncologists were unanimous: she required immediate surgery. They gave her a terrifying ultimatum—without the operation, she had two weeks to live.

Desperate and terrified, Lela went to Samtavro. She stood before the grave of the man who had promised to answer the prayers of those who sought him. There, she experienced a vision. "Fr. Gabriel was standing there and smiling at me," she recounted.

That smile communicated a reassurance that medical science could not offer. Filled with sudden faith, Lela made a decision that defied all medical advice: she refused the operation. Instead, she began to visit the grave regularly, anointing herself with the oil from the lampada.

Two months later, she returned to the doctors for an examination. The medical team prepared to see a woman in the final stages of terminal decline. Instead, the scans revealed a clean system. "Nothing resembling a tumor was found," Lela testified. The deadline of death had passed, and she was alive, healed by the smile of a saint and a drop of oil.

The Beard of the Priest

Pelagea Tamarashvili, from the village of Saguramo, suffered from a fibroma and myoma. Her illness was so severe that she would periodically lose her ability to speak. A relative brought her a vial of Father Gabriel's oil. Pelagea anointed herself twice and felt relief. But as she prepared for the third anointing, her symptoms flared; she felt her speech slipping away again.

Discouraged, she gave in to doubt. "It doesn't help," she told herself, putting the oil away and going to sleep without prayer.

That night, the Elder paid her a house call in her dreams. A priest with a large beard appeared to her. He did not offer sympathy for her doubt; he offered a rebuke for her lack of spiritual effort.

"Here you are lamenting, 'It doesn't help, it doesn't help'— but what can help you, if you haven't prayed?" the figure in the dream scolded her. "Pray, and you will see whether it helps or not. Look at me. I am a priest, and I have a beard. Would I have a beard unless I were a priest? You say that you believe, but you don't pray—what kind of faith is that? Pray, and you will have help."

Pelagea woke up with the sting of the rebuke fresh in her mind. She resumed the anointing, but this time she coupled it with fervent prayer. The result was absolute. A subsequent ultrasound showed that the fibroma and myoma had vanished. The doctor, she noted, "nearly went crazy out of amazement."

The Impossible Biology

The healings were not limited to tumors. Vano Tsilikashvili suffered from total bone marrow fibrosis. His condition was horrific; a yellow liquid was leaking from his bones, signaling the total collapse of his body's structural integrity. The doctors had lost hope, sending him home to die.

Vano turned to the oil. He anointed himself and drank it. Three months later, he was not only alive but completely healthy. But the healing came with a bizarre, visual signature of the saint's power. Before the illness, Vano had grey hair and eyebrows. After taking the oil, his eyebrows turned black, and his hair became dark with grey streaks. It was a reversal of aging, a biological "rewind" orchestrated by grace.

Suliko Gvinjilia from Senaki suffered from cirrhosis of the liver in its most serious form. On November 4, 2004, she visited the grave, anointed herself, and asked for a blessing to be admitted to the hospital, which had previously refused her. When she returned, she was admitted. The ultrasound scan revealed a liver that showed no trace of cirrhosis. The irreversible scarring had been reversed.

The Prisoners' Saint

Perhaps most poignant were the miracles that occurred behind bars. Father Gabriel, who had been Prisoner #666, became the patron of the incarcerated.

Vasiliy Narindoshvili, serving a sentence in the Ksanskaya Colony, suffered from a ruptured eardrum caused by beatings in 1994-1995. Blood and pus drained constantly from his ear, and he was deaf on that side. He anointed his ear twice with the oil. The pain vanished, and 80-90% of his hearing returned.

Vasiliy became a conduit for the oil's power within the prison. When a woman visited the prison with her 10-month-old son, the baby fell severely ill with a high fever. The doctors were helpless. The prisoners sent for Vasiliy. The weakened baby reached out to the prisoner. Vasiliy put a drop of oil on the baby's pinky finger and made the sign of the Cross on his forehead. The child licked the oil from his finger, fell asleep, and woke up completely healthy.

Another prisoner, Artur Soukasyan, had a foot that was festering and rotting, with two toes in a state of necrosis. Nothing helped. Vasiliy anointed the foot with oil and sprinkled it with earth from Father Gabriel's grave. The next morning, when Artur took off the bandage, the rot was gone. The foot was healthy. The "white ticket" monk was liberating them from their physical prisons, even as they remained behind bars.

The Miracle of the Jacket

While the grave at Samtavro was the epicenter of veneration, another relic appeared in a different location, offering a more tactile connection to the saint. In the **Monastery of the Nativity of the Most Holy Mother of God**, the nuns kept a jacket that had belonged to Father Gabriel. It was the simple garment he had worn under his monastic mantle.

This jacket was not kept behind glass. It was accessible. Pilgrims discovered that the nuns allowed them to wear it. One pilgrim from Russia described the experience of finding this relic. Having heard two women discussing "Mama Gabrieli's jacket," she rushed to the church. A nun helped her put it on. From the left pocket hung a little silver cross on a chain.

For the pilgrim, wearing the jacket was not merely a sentimental act; it was a spiritual encounter. She described staying at the monastery for several days, during which "a great number of unbelievable things happened." Every morning, while the monastery gates were still closed, she would go to the church, put on the saint's jacket, and read her morning prayers, wrapped in the warmth of the Confessor.

In the evenings, the jacket became a communal source of comfort. The sisters would gather in the reception room near the refectory. They would take turns sitting at the table with the jacket thrown over their shoulders. It was a shared grace, passed from nun to nun with the playful admonition: "Look, you've already worn it—give it to me now".

Through the blood that refused to clot, the oil that burned tumors, and the jacket that warmed the shoulders of the faithful, Saint Gabriel continued his ministry. He remained the "Mama Gabrieli" of the people—accessible, miraculous, and overwhelmingly alive. As he had promised in his last testament: "I carry away with me love for everyone... I will not leave you." And indeed, he has not.

Chapter 13

Stories About Saint Gabriel

The Circle of Judgment

One summer afternoon, a young artist and his companions gathered outside the gates of Samtavro Monastery, their voices mingling in the warm Georgian air. Five or six of them had clustered together, drawn into one of those conversations that feels both urgent and uncertain.

The subject was Father Gabriel—specifically, his habit of performing somersaults during the Divine Liturgy.

"Look, we know he's a saint," one of them said, gesturing emphatically. "But the others don't know this. What must they think?"

Another nodded in agreement. "There are limits, surely. The liturgy is sacred. How can he do such things? While the service is going on, he's doing God knows what."

The artist listened as his friends debated, each adding their own concerns to the growing chorus of doubt. They formed a tight circle, their heads bent together in conspiratorial conversation, oblivious to the world around them.

Then a taxi pulled up to the curb.

The door opened, and out stepped the Elder himself. Without hesitation, he walked directly toward the circle of young men. They didn't notice him until he was upon them.

Father Gabriel thrust his head into the center of their circle, his eyes moving from face to face. The question he posed was simple, direct, and devastating:

"Are you judging me?"

Silence fell like a stone. The artist and his friends stood frozen, mouths half-open, words dying on their tongues. Not one of them could find a reply.

The Elder waited only a moment, his gaze holding them in place. Then, as calmly as he had arrived, he turned and walked away, leaving them to contemplate the weight of their own words.

The Cup of Wisdom

One day, a group of young men set out to visit Elder Gabriel's hermitage, eager to receive a blessing from the holy monk. When they arrived at his dwelling, they were met with an unexpected sight: the Saint stood in front of his cell, swaying drunkenly, a bottle in one hand and a cup in the other.

Father Gabriel spotted them and called the young men closer. Before their eyes, he poured himself a glass and downed it in one gulp.

He continued his performance, toasting and drinking cup after cup while dispensing advice to his visitors. The scene was bewildering, yet something remarkable was happening. Each young man heard the words Father Gabriel was saying differently—each hearing something beneficial said specifically for him, as though the Elder knew the precise need of every soul standing before him.

But one of the young men was especially disturbed by the monk's behavior. He watched with growing disapproval, his face darkening as he glared angrily at the swaying figure before them.

As the group prepared to leave, Father Gabriel's demeanor suddenly changed. His face became very serious and sober. He called over the upset young man.

The Elder handed him a full cup and said lovingly, "Have a cup, my dear one."

The young man hesitated, then took a small sip. He was stunned. What touched his lips was not wine at all, but cherry juice diluted with water.

Father Gabriel's eyes held his. "Don't judge any of God's creations," he said. "If I start judging you and consider I am better than you, I will be abominable before the Lord. Remember this, my dear one, and go in peace."

The young man departed in silence, carrying with him a lesson far more potent than any cup of wine.

The Unspoken Desire

A woman once came to Father Gabriel with a request that startled those present. She asked if he might give her an icon—a bold petition, for everyone knew how dearly the Elder treasured each sacred image in his cell. Yet without hesitation, Father Gabriel rose and took down not only an icon from the wall, but a cross as well, placing both in her hands.

The woman stood speechless for a moment, then fell to her knees at his feet. "You have read my very thoughts!" she cried. "wanted so much to have a cross also, Thank you very much!" Tears of gratitude streamed down her face as she thanked him again and again.

The Elder had perceived what lay unspoken in her heart, answering not only the request she voiced, but the deeper desire she had kept silent.

Conversations with Angels

It was six o'clock in the evening when a nun sat keeping vigil with Father Gabriel in his cell. Without warning, the Elder turned to her and said, "Leave me alone now. I am not to be watched."

Confused by the sudden dismissal, she asked, "Why, Father?"

"Leave me," he repeated, turning his face away from her.

As she rose and took a few steps toward the door, something made her glance back. The Elder's face had become radiant, illuminated as though catching beams of sunlight—yet there was no natural light that could account for such brightness.

This same nun had been granted a rare privilege: she was permitted to enter Father Gabriel's cell without first saying the customary prayer. On another occasion, she made the sign of the cross and quietly opened his door. Inside, she heard the Elder speaking with someone in earnest conversation. Yet when she looked about the small cell, she found him utterly alone.

"Father, to whom are you speaking?" she asked.

He turned to her with perfect simplicity and replied, "To angels."

The Elder's Protection

A woman once came to Father Gabriel to thank him for saving her life. She told the following story:

"I live near the cemetery in a small abandoned house. One night robbers rushed in by breaking the door. I was frightened and started calling Father Gabriel for help. Father Gabriel appeared all of a sudden holding a truncheon in his hand. The robbers vanished immediately and Father Gabriel disappeared with them."

The Descent of the Holy Spirit

A clergyman once asked Father Gabriel whether the coming down of the Holy Spirit is visible.

The Elder answered: "It looks like two small circles appearing in the form of fire flies, making circular rotations that gradually grow bigger and brighter. At this moment the Holy Spirit is descending on you and you become filled with Holy Spirit. You have a feeling you possess the universe, you are able to see everything that going on around; even if the whole army or the whole world is raised against you, you will overpower them without any effort."

The Gift of a Child

A young couple came to Father Gabriel in distress. They had been married for many years but had no children, and the doctors offered little hope.

Father Gabriel made them kneel down, blessed them, and gave them specific instruction: they were to perform three Supplication Services to Saint John the Baptist, and their prayers would be heard. He calmed the anxious woman and assured her she would be a mother within a year.

"If it is a boy, we'll give him your name," she said with a happy smile.

"Why, Queen Tamar was a woman but wasn't she superior?" the Elder replied.

A year later, the couple returned carrying their long-awaited baby Maria to be blessed by the Elder.

The Sealed Blessing

One day a priest brought his spiritual son to Father Gabriel for blessing. The young man was preparing to be tonsured as a monk.

The priest asked Father Gabriel what he thought of the novice. The Elder fixed his gaze upon the young man, then suddenly embraced him and said: "You can tonsure him right away."

The novice was tonsured, but soon afterward his faith was shattered and he fell into apostasy, abandoning the monastery and the church.

Yet in time, he returned. Those who knew the story were certain it was Father Gabriel's prayers that brought him back and helped him regain his faith. By transferring Divine Grace through his embrace, the Elder had sealed the young man's faith forever, ensuring that even in his darkest moment of doubt, the way back would remain open to him.

It is known from the life of Saint Simeon the Fool-for-Christ that the saint would hug people to seal God's grace upon them. Father Gabriel, in his spiritual wisdom, had done the same.

The Test of Faith

Once a hieromonk came to Father Gabriel and boldly declared that he did not believe in his miracles.

"Kneel down," the Elder ordered. The hieromonk knelt reverently before him.

"And now I bless you to rise to your feet, if you can," said Father Gabriel.

"Can you imagine," the hieromonk recalled later, "I wanted to rise to my feet, but I could not!"

Deliverance from Discord

A girl came to Father Gabriel complaining of constant quarrels in the family. Her brother had run out of the house in anger, and she feared he would not return.

Without delay, the Elder went with the girl to her home. As they entered the room, they found the brother already there. When asked how he had returned, he explained that some invisible force had brought him back.

Father Gabriel came up to the icon of the Holy Virgin and began to pray, raising his hands to Heaven. As the girl recalled, his face was flooded with Divine radiance and his prayers were so powerful that the spell cast upon the family was driven out of their house. Finally, rest and peace were established forever in their home.

The Elder's Watchful Care

Nun Nana (Kutateladze) recalled that Father Gabriel didn't like to let the nuns leave the Convent. Once she and her sisters left for some errands without his blessing. They were joking and laughing, thinking they had managed to slip away and were out of the Elder's reach.

When they thought they had left him far behind, all of a sudden he appeared before them to their great astonishment. They didn't know he possessed God-blessed prophetic power and that it was impossible to conceal anything from him. Though he said nothing, they saw fatherly care in his stern look.

Driving Away the Mockers

Early on, a man asked Father Gabriel to sanctify his dwelling.

When the priest arrived, boys who had been playing near the house began to mock him, crying out: "Hey, Blackcoat! Blackcoat!"

Father Gabriel responded by raising his hands as if in dance and lifting the hem of his robe, shouting: "I'll show you chanticleers!"

The boys stood dumbfounded. They exchanged glances with one another and muttered, "He is not normal," then ran away in confusion.

When asked why he had acted in such an unusual manner, Father Gabriel explained simply that there was no other way to get rid of them.

Dear Reader,

I am by no means a professional non-fiction writer, but I spent a lot of time , love, and effort on this book.

When I first started, I didn't understand the magnitude of taking on non-fiction. Needless to say, I have a lot more respect for authors in this field now.

I can't ask any more of you. You have read my book. That alone is wonderful. But I would humbly request that if you enjoyed this book at all, you might consider leaving a review on Amazon or wherever you night have purchased it. It really does go a long way.

Thank you for taking this journey with me, and Christ Keep You All.

James Mamone
12/14/25

Appendices

Aphorisms of the Elder

Saint Gabriel of Georgia left behind no manuscripts, no carefully edited volumes of spiritual instruction.

He said, "I never wrote down anything. He [God] wrote in people's thoughts."

He was not a man of the written word—he was a man of the living encounter, and his teachings existed only in the moment they were spoken, breathed into the air between himself and the soul standing before him.

Yet nothing was lost.

Those who came to him carried his words away like hidden treasure, each syllable settling deep into memory, taking root in the fertile soil of transformed hearts. What he gave them was not doctrine to be memorized but fire to be kindled, and it burned on long after he spoke.

The Elder spent himself utterly. Every ounce of strength—physical, mental, spiritual—he poured out for those who sought him. He worked as a man works who knows that souls hang in the balance, that a single word spoken in season might turn a life from darkness toward unquenchable light. How many he rescued from despair's edge, how many he pulled back from the precipice of pride and emptiness, only God knows.

For truth does not age. The words that guided seekers in Soviet Georgia still speak to hearts today, wherever genuine hunger for God is found. What follows is a sharing of that inheritance, offered to all whose souls are awake enough to recognize light when they see it.

I have done my best, in the most minimal effort, to correct some of the translations that I have found, and correct syntax. Nothing else has been changed, and if there was a question as to intent, I left it as is.

These fragments—sharp, clear, carrying the authority of lived holiness—are what we have. And they are enough.

* * *

Love everyone; if you can't, at least show goodwill.

Meekness is an ever-lit God-pleasing candle.

Death is transfiguration. Don't be afraid of death; rather, be afraid of the Judgement Day.

How to love a malicious person? By hating evil. By God's will, a man inflicting evil now, through lamentation, fasting, and repentance, some day may be purged of sin and turn into an angel.

Without God's will, not even bread crumbs fall down.

A humbled man is protected from temptations. No one can enter the Kingdom of God without humbleness.

Seas dry up, mountains collapse, but the glory of Christ remains forever.

Your soul belongs to the One Who bestowed it to you.

Have a kind disposition towards your fellow men; as for helping a man in need, it requires wisdom, which is God's gift—it is a kind of sacrifice made to God.

When mentioning the name of the Lord your God, get up and make the sign of the cross.

Love each other. Georgia will be saved by love. We are witnessing the last age. You will see the Antichrist. The Lord our God will demand love for God and neighbor; whoever holds out to the end will be saved.

If you don't fall, you will never rise and feel repentance. I am a great sinner myself; that's why I have a special feeling of compassion for all sinners.

Christ was recognized by His humbleness and wisdom.

Do you want to be saved? Hasten to give alms and have brotherly love towards your fellow men.

The last time a man will be saved is by love, humbleness, and kindness. Kindness will open the gates of Heaven; humbleness will lead into Heaven; the man whose heart is filled with love will see God.

Even if you hate only one person, in his image you hate Christ Himself; therefore, you are too far from the Heavenly Kingdom.

If you possess everything but love, consider you possess nothing. Love dominates all rules and laws.

Never lose hope for God's Providence.

When you do something good, you ascend one step up; when you sin, you descend one step down. Our life consists of such ups and downs.

A man is put to the test by Holy Providence as admitted by God.

Christ didn't walk on roads laid with carpets. He was simple; hypocrisy and pomposity were repulsive to Him. Christ wore only one tunic knitted by the Holy Mother of God.

God is infinite Love, Goodness, and Justice. Whoever loves goodness and justice loves God, and he is loved by God as His own child. It is not God who abandons a man, but a man who abandons God. Hades is estrangement from God.

It doesn't do for the Christian to moan.

Denounce a man with love.

Consciousness is a small particle of God in your heart.

We think we possess love. But what is love, and how do we perceive it? According to Apostle Paul: "Love is patient, love is kind. It does not envy, it does not boast, it is not proud. It is not rude, it is not self-seeking, it is not easily angered, it keeps no record of wrongs. Love does not delight in evil but rejoices with the truth. It always protects, always trusts, always hopes, always perseveres" (1 Corinthians 13:4-7). This is genuine love on which the happiness of mankind rests. Love is the greatest virtue, but it is still more important to learn how to love. Without sacrifice for the sake of God and neighbor, neither spiritual heights nor love can be achieved.

Have you sinned? Repent immediately!

When having meals, remember those who are in need: hungry, thirsty, suffering—this way you learn how to draw upon Divine grace.

When you go in for an examination before your professor, your heart starts palpitating; imagine how you will feel before the Creator. The greatness of God is incomparable.

For God, all sins are like sea pebbles. There exists no sin that may surpass God's compassion.

How can a man's soul be calm if his neighbor is in danger? If someone is sick at home and there is no one to take care of him, it's better not to attend the church service but to stay at home and show affection toward the neighbor.

Egoism is opposed to love. An egoist never gives anything away; he wants only to get. Even all the riches of the world are not sufficient for him.

If to save a sick neighbor, you are determined to go far away at night, through a dense wood, irrespective of all dangers, and bring him medicine—this is love for the neighbor.

It is difficult for a man to perceive the meaning of Providence. There are three events ascribed to Divine interposition: Admission, the Will of God, and Providence. Admission means that a man is given free will by God to do whatever he wants. By the Will of God, a man does whatever God commands him to do; it is always beneficial and aimed at saving man's soul. Providence means the care exercised by God to control Admission and Will. If you find the problem too difficult to solve, entrust it to Providence and don't think about it anymore.

Man must bless his path with reasonable decisions. His path depends on the way he acts. God has endowed man with free will. Who am I to interfere?

The eye is a mirror of your soul. Should it be against the soul's will, you would never look at anything wrong.

Idle talk is offensive to God. Kind deeds mean love for your neighbor.

We must repent with our hearts rather than shed tears.

Love your enemy—it is clear. But how do we love Christ's enemy? Stop hating him, and then you will be able to love him.

Conscience is a small God. Before going to bed, render a short account to yourself: how you spent the day, what you did, when you sinned, and what should have been done. Be demanding toward yourself.

Someone may say it was his fate. There is no fate. If his fate was to die and it was determined beforehand, why is he to be judged on the Day of Judgment? We create our fate ourselves. If a man, out of his recklessness, puts his life at risk, what does that have to do with fate?

Love will tame even the fiercest lion.

If you are slandered or your good deed is repaid with evil, bear no malice in your heart. Forgive the slanderer and rejoice that you have ascended toward God by a few steps.

Faith and love are perceived through suffering.

Will everyone be saved? No. God is merciful but not to all; nobody can help you unless you strive for your salvation. Whoever saves his soul and helps his neighbor by word or deed obeys the commandments of God. Having free will, you must strive for salvation.

The first healer is God, the next one is a doctor, but the one who gives no thanks to the doctor gives no thanks to God. The worker is to be rewarded. The hands and mind of a doctor perform God-pleasing deeds.

He who exalts himself will be humbled, and he who humbles himself will be exalted.

Mercy is gold; humbleness is a diamond.

A man striving for kind deeds for the sake of his neighbor is striving to save his own soul.

Do not use the name of the Lord your God in vain; if you do, you break the third commandment.

The Lord our God demands a pure heart and kind deeds from us.

Try to strive for God constantly. Having seen your aspiration for God, the Lord will grant you all that is necessary.

The righteous do not have the fear of God.

The spirit comprises three faculties: rational, emotional, and volitional. The rational is in man's mind, the emotional is in his heart, and the volitional is in his body. The immortal spirit, contrary to animals and birds, involves the fear of God, conscience, and strivings for God. The immortal spirit is in the blood, but it is not only blood. Before the Fall, the soul and body submitted to the spirit. After the Fall, communication with the spirit was interrupted, and the soul remained under volitional control. Whatever wish the volitional faculty has, the same will is exercised by the soul. The soul dislocates, and the spirit intellectualizes the mind through consciousness. For the salvation of a man, God gave him a conscience, which allows man to distinguish good from bad. This is the reason why sometimes we have a feeling of joy or dislike towards a passing stranger.

A monk must have a steadfast spirit; he has to struggle for the truth, as the truth is God Himself.

The monk should fatigue himself with physical work. He will be saved by toiling.

To approach a monk means to play with fire.

True faith finds its place in a man's heart, not in his mind. The Antichrist will be disclosed by believers who have their faith in *their hearts; those with their faith in their minds will follow the Antichrist.*

Never try to excuse yourself, and do not do anything of your own will.

Morals and manners are changing in Georgia. Those carried away by worldly temptations will be easily recognized: they will walk naked. The way a person is dressed reflects his spiritual state. A Christian's clothing will be modest. According to the Holy Church canons, a woman wearing a man's dress is condemned.

For the Lord, it is not so important whether you are a monk or a layman; what is important is to have a thirst for God. Through this thirst, a man can be saved. The monk will be judged by monastic canons, while the secular will be judged by worldly rules.

Woe to those who will try to interpret the Holy Testament in their own way. Later, the followers of the Antichrist will also attend church, make the sign of the cross, and preach the Holy Testament. Genuine believers will be recognized by kind deeds.

Don't leave the monastery for a long time.

If you want to be a monk, you are already a monk.

Monasticism is a celestial order. To achieve perfection, you have to pass through the fire of temptations.

Half of Hell is already on Earth. The Antichrist was already born; he is at the door, not knocking, but breaking in. You will witness his reign. His seal will be made visible on the forehead and arms.

If you steal food, you will break one of the commandments; this way, you will become the Antichrist's follower. The believers will be entrusted to God.

A monk must live a simple life. God's grace is in simplicity.

The monk, too, needs compassion and consolation.

The Antichrist will not be enthroned in Georgia, and the persecutions here will be considerably less severe. Woe to those who try to interpret the Holy Testament in their own way. Later, the Antichrist's followers will also attend church, make the sign of the cross, and preach the Holy Testament. Genuine believers will be recognized by their kind deeds.

In order to be saved, don't be excessively concerned with your body, but rather with your soul. Whoever conquers the tongue and gluttony is already on the right path.

The seal will be put on the forefinger, not on the palm. It will be invisible; it will be placed under the skin with the help of the computer. First, the seal will be offered to volunteers. However, with the enthronement of the Antichrist, everyone will be pressured to accept the seal. Disobedience will be claimed a treachery. People will flee to the woods. Precautions should be taken to move in groups of about ten to fifteen, as the demon might try to nudge them from the cliffs. The believers will be protected by the Holy Spirit. Whatever happens, never lose hope. Help each other. God will open your mind, and you will know how to react. The one who endures will be saved. No true believer will feel either hunger or thirst. In times of disaster, he will not wither. The Lord will work miracles for them. One leaf of a plant will provide enough food for a month. By making the sign of the cross, a lump of earth will be changed into bread.

It's impossible to be saved without grief.

Some food products have already been sealed, but it doesn't matter. Before taking meals, you have to say the Lord's Prayer, make the sign of the cross, and sprinkle the food with sanctified water. Don't take bread from a person who has accepted the antichrist's seal.

Never betray God. Endure all trials, and the gates of the Heavens will be opened for you.

Remember, your spiritual father is always with you and watches each step you take.

A good monk will content himself with prosphora only.

Even if an angel himself appears before you in his splendid grandeur, do not do anything without blessing; never change the blessing given by your spiritual father.

Woe to a monk who does not share the anguish of his own people.

Georgia will be enlightened in the last age, and it will be revealed not materially but spiritually. Believers from many countries will gather in Georgia. The wicked deeds started by the communists are only a prologue. The main events are coming. From time immemorial, the world has never witnessed such sorrow. And this is the end. Georgia will be protected by the Holy Virgin, as Iberia is the country chosen by the Holy Mother of God as Her lot. The fight between the prophets Enoch, Elias, and the antichrist will be shown on TV. The leaving of the Holy Mountain by the icon of the Iberian Holy Virgin will be followed by bell ringing, and churches will bow to commemorate the farewell. This will also be shown on TV, so that the whole world can see it and those who want to save their souls can come to Georgia.

A monastery is not a hotel; it is a big vessel of love.

Impertinent is the one who does not see his transgressions and boasts of himself. Those whose hearts are filled with pride and vain glory are loathsome before God.

During the antichrist's times, the strongest temptation will be the anticipation of salvation from the cosmos, from "humanoids," "extraterrestrials," which are actually masks of demons. The struggler of prayer should rarely look up at the sky, as the signs might be deceptive, and he may be ruined.

To be saved, monks must live according to the Gospel; the seculars must obey the Ten Commandments.

The coming of the antichrist had been anticipated before; there were wars also, but there were neither signs from Heaven nor general apostasy.

Monastic grace is lost in the world.

Satan has spread 666 traps. His seal will be made not only invisibly but also visibly on the forehead and arms. If the seal impression is made by force, in God's sight, it will be considered like a virgin disgraced. The hardest trial for Christians will be their relatives who accepted the seal. The seal won't take effect if made against someone's will. But imagine the trap set by the Antichrist for a mother left with five children. How to feed them if she does not accept the seal?

If a monk has no humbleness and penitence, there is no salvation for him.

There is no greater heroism than monasticism.

A monk, like a roaring lion, must uphold the Orthodox faith.

Praise may ruin the monk. The one who praises a monk is his enemy.

Monasticism is a combat; strive for God till the last breath.

If you consider yourself to have risen above others, you are loathsome before God.

A monk cannot be carefree; he is Christ's warrior.

Remember: Christ is the only One; there will never be another.

If a layman overcomes his passions due to Christ, he is placed on the same footing as a monk.

To become wise, first, you must be stupid.

If you never fell, you will never perceive the Lord's power. Should I be faultless, how could I love God?

The Orthodox Church is a ship sailing over the rough and stormy ocean. The Orthodox Christians are the passengers of the ship, while people of other religions are swimmers in the open sea.

A hegumenos has to denounce spiritual children to reveal their faults. If they disobey, God is their judge.

Failing to keep one's word is a grave sin.

You have to choose your spiritual father of your own will; but having chosen him, show complete obedience to him. If his teachings are heretical, flee from him as from fire.

A mentally diseased person who committed suicide will be forgiven by God. However, a person who intentionally took his life goes to Hades. We cannot pray for them, but to help them, we have to give alms and perform good deeds in the name of the departed. Sometimes they are brought out of Hades.

If you witness someone being robbed and you can't do anything, start saying the Lord's Prayer.

The more grace, the greater the reward.

Resemble a child by purity of heart and innocence, but not by mind.

The Heavenly Kingdom is the most blessed domain of God. On earth, by its sanctity after Jerusalem, comes Sveti-Tskhovely, and then the Samtavro Convent of Saint Nino, where the Equal-to-the-Apostles Saint was preaching with the Cross made of vine, given by the Holy Virgin.

Faith is God's blessed talent.

Great holiness possesses God-gifted grace, having a circle around it. No evil is able to approach such a circle.

When the demon captures a man, first he deprives him of his mind.

God's grace has always been with the Georgian Orthodox Church. The endless chain of saints has never been broken and will never break.

For physical and spiritual strength, take holy water and prosphora with trust and reverence.

Who does not rejoice in Holy Week but cries over his sins behaves like Judas.

If you see a killer, a whore, or a drunkard prostrated on the ground, never judge them, since their bridles have been loosened by God while yours are held firm. If God sets free your rein, you will find yourself in a worse condition and commit the sin which you had condemned, and get ruined. Just as a thread passes through the needle's eye, the same way you have to pass through the sin you have committed.

In worshiping the icons, touch or kiss the icon case, but not the image.

Any kind of transgression is a display of hostility towards God. Think for a moment—whom are you wrestling with?

If your faith has been abused in your presence and you kept silent, you are worse than the abuser.

Georgia will rise like Lazarus through many hardships and sufferings, but not until the restoration of the monarchy. Salvation will come when you feel: "This is the End."

Have only one fear—not to sin.

How to pray for your enemies? First, pray for those whom you love more, for example your children. Then pray for the other members of your family, then for your neighbors and relatives, in order to avoid having enemies. Bless the town where you live, not only Tbilisi but all cities of Georgia. Since there is not only Georgia but also other countries around it, ask God to avert hostility from peoples. Now that you prayed for everyone, only your enemy remains. Ask God to fill his heart with kindness and his mind with wisdom. This way, you will be able to pray for your enemies.

Your trials are due to your little faith. Ask God to forgive you and strengthen your faith.

Don't accept an offering of "Judas's money." With such money, you will be involved in sin from which it is rather difficult to recover.

Stealing is a sin, but stealing sacred items is a graver sin.

When you condemn someone, you condemn God.

God's wrath is upon women who have had an abortion. Repent and pray constantly so that God may forgive your sin of slaughtering your own children.

Don't give advice to your neighbor if you do not know his spiritual state. Your advice may aggravate his state to such an extent that it could ruin him.

You have to refer to the Elder in case of spiritual need, for edification, and to learn wisdom.

Thank God that you were born Orthodox in faith. Display steadfast spirit; do not be tempted by concerns about whether people of other religions will be saved or not. This is not our prerogative but God's unfailing love.

Be concerned with your own business, not with others' transgressions. Sit and cry over your own sins.

He who gives unjust orders is more sinful than the one who executes them.

If a person is overwhelmed by his lust but he suppresses it due to the love for Christ, he is crowned with glory.

The blessing descends upon a person at his birthplace.

If prayers are not followed by kind deeds, the prayers are dead.

Correct your fellow man once, twice, three times; if rejected, leave him.

You condemn someone for having sinned. But have you seen that he repented and God absolved him?

It is bad when your tongue runs ahead while your mind lags behind.

Your soul dies when you do nothing to defend your faith; but when you die to defend your faith, the door to the Kingdom of Heaven opens before you.

To place pictures of icons in daily newspapers is a crime.

You cannot demand much of a person if you never gave him anything.

Outrage and impudence are the origin of any transgression.

When someone raises prayers before the icons or crosses made by you, half of the blessing comes upon you.

Your benevolences or fervent prayers should be given to God as your sacrifice.

The Cross borne by the Catholicos-Patriarch of Georgia is very heavy. Who judges him puts burning charcoal on his own head.

Do not always trust your eyes and ears — you might be deceived.

Never judge; the only Judge is God. Who condemns resembles an empty ear of wheat, whose head is always uplifted.

Never worship a worldly man.

A child in its mother's womb can hear everything. Be careful as to your words and behavior; choose God's words, as upbringing starts from the first day the child is brought to life.

If while saying prayers you are asked for help and you say, "Let me first finish the prayers and then I'll help you," your prayers are of no use.

The face of the Lord is turned away from those who hate meat and bread.

Say prayers with profound reverence; consider before whom you are standing, whom you are talking to. Christ is always invisibly with us.

Ecumenism is a super heresy. It is better to be a streetwalker than to be addicted to heresy.

All sinners who repent are God's children; they are admitted to receive the Holy Communion.

To live with no faith in God and beyond the Church is equal to blasphemy.

If you do not obey God's commandments, do not bother the Lord with your long prayers; they will not be heard.

Denounce your neighbor, but do not condemn, as it is quite different.

The Medical Verdict

Full text of the 1965 psychiatric conclusion (Patient #666)

Georgian SSR Tbilisi Healthcare City Psycho-Neurological Hospital 19/1 – 1966, Tbilisi, 1, Electroni Str. #666

Patient: Vassili Urgebadze, born in 1929, 6 class education. Address: 11, Tetritskaro Str.

The patient was admitted to the city psycho-neurological hospital on August 18th, 1965, brought from prison for compulsory treatment.

Diagnosis: Psychopathic individual prone to schizophrenia-like blank episodes. He was discharged from the hospital on November 19th, 1965.

According to his medical history, he experienced visions of a ghostly evil spirit with horns on its head at the age of 12... The patient contends that all the evils in the world are the result of malevolent forces. He began attending churches, engaging in prayer, acquiring icons, and studying church literature from the age of 12... He observed fasting on Wednesdays and Fridays. Adults and soldiers ridiculed his beliefs: "On Wednesday, Judas sold Christ for 30 pieces of silver, and on

Friday, Jewish priests crucified him." His thoughts appeared to be entirely hallucinatory.

It became evident from the case that on May 1st, 1965, during a demonstration, he set fire to a large portrait of Lenin hanging on the Council of Ministers building. After an interrogation, he explained that he did this because he believed a depiction of the Crucifixion of Christ should adorn that spot, rather than idolizing a mere mortal man. This raised doubts about his mental well-being, leading to his referral for a court-ordered psychopathic evaluation.

The assessment revealed that the patient's orientation was disoriented with respect to time, place, and environment. He engaged in whispered self-talk, expressing belief in the existence of heavenly beings, God, angels, etc. Throughout conversation, his focus consistently centered on the concept that everything was subject to God's will, etc. He was isolated from other patients in the ward. When engaged in conversation, he surely mentioned God, angels, and icons. He displayed an inability to critically assess his condition. He received treatment involving aminazine-phrazia and symptomicine therapy, following which he underwent a medical review.

Act of stationary #42 1965

Chairman of the commission: candidate of medicine, chief physician T. Abramishvili, **Members:** J. Shalamberidze and physician Kropov.

He was discharged from the hospital on 19 Jan, 1965 and was taken home by his mother.

Physician: Lezhava. 19 Jan. 1966.

Sources

- **Birth and Early Childhood:** The details regarding Goderdzi's birth on August 26, 1929, the murder of his father Vasil when Goderdzi was two years old, and the family's use of the nickname "Vasiko" are derived from "Elder's Diadem", "Life and works", and "The Canadian Journal of Orthodox Christianity".

  - **Childhood Piety and Eccentricities:** The accounts of Vasiko building small churches from pebbles and lighting matches inside them, as well as his habit of running with a stick while birds followed him and his refusal to use mousetraps, are found in "Life and works" and "The Canadian Journal of Orthodox Christianity".

  - **The Purchase of the Gospel:** The pivotal moment when Vasiko heard neighbors arguing ("You have crucified me like Christ") and his subsequent purchase of the Gospel after saving money are recounted in "Elder's Diadem", "OrthoChristian", and "Saint Silouan Orthodox Church".

  - **The Vision of the Cross:** The description of the twelve-year-old Vasiko standing on his balcony and seeing a large cross in the sky is detailed in "Life and works" and "The Canadian Journal of Orthodox Christianity".

- **The Demonic Attack:** The account of the demon appearing with a "terrible face," striking Vasiko, and his subsequent strengthening of faith ("if the Demon exists, then God exists in even greater measure") is sourced from "Life and works" and "The Canadian Journal of Orthodox Christianity".

- **Uncle Mukha and the Boulder:** The story of the neighbor Uncle Mukha (George) being unable to lift the boulder at the ruined St. George church, and Vasiko lifting it "in the name of Christ," is drawn from "Life and works" and "The Canadian Journal of Orthodox Christianity".

- **Collecting Icons:** Vasiko's practice of confronting neighbors who had hidden their icons and offering to keep them safe is described in "Life and works" and "The Canadian Journal of Orthodox Christianity".

- **Military Service and Fasting:** The details regarding Goderdzi's conscription into the Soviet Army in 1949, his service in the Batumi border guard unit, and his secret visits to St. Nicholas Church are found in "Life and works" [Source 4] and "The Life of the Venerable Gabriel" [Source 10]. The specific detail that he fasted on Wednesdays and Fridays under the pretext of having stomach pains to avoid eating non-lenten army rations is derived from "The Life of the Venerable Gabriel" [Source 10].

- **The "White Ticket" and Diagnosis:** The account of his interrogation regarding childhood visions (specifically the demon at age 12) upon returning from the army, and the subsequent issuance of a "white ticket" (certificate of mental illness) and a Class II disability pension to prevent him from holding a job, is detailed in "Life and works" [Source 4] and "The Life of the Venerable Gabriel" [Source 10].

- **Building the Backyard Church:** The construction

of the church in his yard on Tetri Tskaro Street using scrap materials is described in "Elder's Diadem" [Source 1], "Ortho-Christian" [Source 2], and "Life and works" [Source 4].

• **Scavenging Icons:** The vivid details of Father Gabriel searching town dumps for discarded icons, cleaning them in his small studio, and framing them with materials like buttons and stones—including framing photos from secular magazines—are sourced from "OrthoChristian" [Source 2] and "The Life of the Venerable Gabriel" [Source 10].

• **Ordination and Monastic Vows:** The involvement of Catholicos-Patriarch Melchizedek III, Goderdzi's service as a watchman and reader at Sioni Cathedral, his tonsure as Monk Gabriel on February 23 (or 27), 1955, and his ordination as Hieromonk by Bishop Gabriel (Chachanidze) are documented in "Elder's Diadem" [Source 1], "Life and works" [Source 4], and "The Life of the Venerable Gabriel" [Source 10].

• **Bethany Monastery:** His service at Bethany Monastery with Fr. George (Mkheidze) and Fr. John (Maisuradze), and the monastery's closure by the government in 1962, are recounted in "Life and works" [Source 4] and "The Life of the Venerable Gabriel" [Source 10].

• **Destruction and Rebuilding of the Church:** The repeated attempts by the government to demolish his back-yard church, his refusal to stop ("I will not destroy the church, if you can, try..."), and the eventual secret apology/pardon from the police chief and party secretary are found in "Elder's Diadem" [Source 1] and "Life and works" [Source 4]. The specific detail about him dismantling the front wall and moving it two meters to appease officials, only to rebuild it larger, is found in "The Life of the Venerable Gabriel" [Source 10].

• **The May Day Demonstration:** The description of the May 1, 1965, demonstration at the Council of Ministers building in Tbilisi, including the 12-meter (or 26-36 foot) high portraits of Lenin and other leaders, is derived from "Elder's Diadem" [Source 1], "Life and works" [Source 4], and "Death to the World" [Source 12].

• **The Act of Burning:** The details of Father Gabriel gaining access (possibly through a window or attic) and pouring kerosene to ignite the banner are found in "Death to the World" [Source 12] and "Life and works" [Source 4].

• **The Sermon from the Window:** The specific proclamation made by Father Gabriel while the portrait burned—"Glory is not due to this dead man, but to Christ the God, who crushed death and gave us eternal life"—is quoted in "Life and works" [Source 4] and "Elder's Diadem" [Source 1]. The variation "Why are you bowing down before idols?" is found in "American Carpatho-Russian" [Source 11] and "Death to the World" [Source 12].

• **The Mob and the Beating:** The account of the crowd attacking him, breaking through barricades, and using rifle butts and fire hoses to beat him is vividly described in "Death to the World" [Source 12]. The specific cry of the mob, "Let me finish off that louse!" is also from "Death to the World" [Source 12].

• **The Injuries and the 8th Regiment:** The fact that the 8th Regiment of the Soviet Internal Forces intervened to save him from being beaten to death is recorded in "Life and works" [Source 4]. The extent of his injuries— seventeen (or eighteen) fractures, including a broken jaw and skull fracture—is documented in "Elder's Diadem" [Source 1], "Life and works" [Source 4], and "Death to the World" [Source 12].

• **Interrogation and the "Beast":** The account of the Soviet authorities offering to spare his life if he confessed to a church conspiracy, his refusal, and his subsequent interrogation where he called Lenin a "beast," leading to further torture, is found in "Life and works" [Source 4].

- **The Medical Verdict and Case #666:** The details regarding his transfer to a psychiatric hospital instead of execution due to international media pressure are found in "Life and works" [Source 4] and "American Carpatho-Russian" [Source 11]. The specific medical diagnosis ("Psychopathic individual... believes in God and angels") and the fact that his case number was listed as **666** are sourced from the full medical report text in "Life and works" [Source 4] and mentioned in "American Carpatho-Russian" [Source 11].

- **Release:** His release after seven months, largely due to the intervention of the renowned Georgian academician Avlip Zurabashvili, is detailed in "Life and works" [Source 4].

- **Release and the "White Ticket":** The details of his release after seven months, largely due to the intervention of Academician Avlip Zurabashvili, and the issuance of the "White Ticket" (certification of mental illness) which prevented him from holding a job, are found in "Life and works" [Source 4] and "OrthoChristian" [Source 2].

- **Suspension from Ministry:** The account of the Church hierarchy suspending him from priestly ministry to appease the Soviet authorities, forbidding him from entering the church or serving, and his practice of receiving Communion as a layman standing in line with the faithful, is documented in "Life and works" [Source 4], "OrthoChristian" [Source 2], and "American Carpatho-Russian" [Source 11].

- **The Decision to become a "Salos":** Father Gabriel's conscious decision to radically change his lifestyle—pretending to be mentally ill, feigning drunkenness, and preaching loudly in the streets to conceal his spiritual gifts and avoid praise—is described in "Life and works" [Source 4] and "American Carpatho-Russian" [Source 11]. The specific quote,

"When it seemed to me that I was an important person or that I was better than others, I would act that way (foolishly); and when people would laugh at me I'd be humbled and see that I'm garbage," is found in "American Carpatho-Russian" [Source 11].

• **The "Drunken" Preaching:** The description of him drinking wine in public to appear as a drunkard, whereas he had previously abstained from alcohol, is found in "Life and works" [Source 4]. The anecdote where he holds a jug of wine covered with a cloth to hide his "weakness" (which was actually a pretense) is mentioned in "Elder's Diadem" [Source 1].

• **Persecution and Poverty:** The details of him being beaten by security officers, sometimes so severely he could not walk, and his family being called to pick him up, are from "Life and works" [Source 4]. The fact that he was a "pariah" avoided by former friends and fellow priests is noted in "American Carpatho-Russian" [Source 11].

• **The "Hen House" Cell:** His move to Samtavro Convent and his residence in a tiny wooden shed that had previously been a chicken coop (hen house) in the "Kaklovani" (walnut alley) is described in "Elder's Diadem" [Source 1], "OrthoChristian" [Source 2], and "Life and works" [Source 4]. The specific details about the shed having 2-3 centimeter gaps in the walls, offering no protection from the winter cold, and his asceticism in living there are found in "Life and works" [Source 4].

• **Restoration to Ministry:** The eventual lifting of his suspension by the Patriarch (specifically mentioned as Patriarch Ephrem II and later Patriarch Ilia II appointing him to Samtavro) is recorded in "Life and works" [Source 4] and "American Carpatho-Russian" [Source 11].

• **"A Man Without Love":** The mention of him wearing a placard around his neck reading "A man without love is like a pitcher without a bottom" is found in "OrthoChristian" [Source 2] and "Saint Silouan Orthodox Church" [Source 12].

• **The "Professor" and Feigning Drunkenness:** The Elder's habit of calling red wine "The Professor" and offering it to guests while pretending to be drunk himself to hide his asceticism (often eating nothing while feeding others) is described in "Elder's Diadem" and "OrthoChristian". The specific detail of him acting foolish or dancing to humble himself when he felt he was being praised is found in "American Carpatho-Russian" and "Elder's Diadem".

• **The Trinity Miracle:** The account of Father Gabriel explaining the Holy Trinity to a visitor (often identified as a Hindu or a follower of Hinduism) by making the sign of the Cross over bread, causing it to separate into fire, water, and wheat, is documented in "Life and works" and "The Life of the Venerable Gabriel".

• **Rebuking the Athonite Abbot:** The encounter with the Athonite monks, specifically Archimandrite Joseph of Xeropotamou, where Father Gabriel rebuked the Abbot for thinking the Virgin Mary had abandoned Georgia, is recounted in "Life and works" and "The Life of the Venerable Gabriel".

• **"My Athos is Here":** His famous reply to the Athonite monks' invitation to move to Mount Athos—"My Athos is here. I would not trade my beloved Georgia for Athos"—is found in "Life and works" and "The Life of the Venerable Gabriel".

• **The Pornographic Magazine Confession:** The story of Father Gabriel instructing a man to buy a pornographic magazine as a penance, thereby revealing the man's secret sin of hiding indecent photographs, is detailed in "American Carpatho-Russian".

• **The Miraculous Car Ride:** The account of the Elder telling a driver (identified as Otar Nikolaishvili or Nun

Elizabeth in different contexts) not to look in the back seat because "Saint Anthony of Martkop is sitting there," followed by the car speeding up supernaturally or the engine cutting out exactly at the destination, is found in "Elder's Diadem", "Ortho-Christian", and "Miraculous Stories".

- **Confronting the Bandits:** The incident where armed men or bandits stopped the car or entered the monastery, and Father Gabriel stepped forward shouting "Shoot me!" causing them to flee in shame or fear, is described in "Elder's Diadem", "OrthoChristian", and "Miraculous Stories".

- **The "Roman Pope" Comment:** The anecdote where he yells at a nun to humble her, then immediately jokes to himself, "Why, the Roman Pope Himself came to me, the sinner, for blessing!" to show the storm had passed, is found in "Elder's Diadem".

- **Final Illness and Dropsy:** The details of the Elder suffering from edema (dropsy) and a broken leg, which left him bedridden for the last year and a half of his life, are found in "Life and works" [Source 4] and "The Life of the Venerable Gabriel" [Source 10]. His refusal to have surgery for his condition is noted in "OrthoChristian" [Source 2].

- **The Miracle of the Incorrupt Blood:** The specific account of the surgeon Zurab Varazashvili (or Varazi) taking 10 ml of blood, the vial breaking and leaving only 2 ml, and the blood being rediscovered years later fresh and incorrupt, leading to its burial in the grave and use for anointing, is detailed in "OrthoChristian" [Source 2] and "Elder's Diadem" [Source 1].

- **Prophecy of Departure:** His statement one day before his death, "The time has come for my departure," and his prayer to the icon of the Savior, "I have followed you, Christ, since the age of 12. I am prepared; take me!" are quoted in "Life and works" [Source 4] and "The Life of the Venerable Gabriel" [Source 10].

• **The Moment of Death:** The details of his final hours —enduring pain until 4:00 AM, calling out "Mother, mother; Sister, sister!", gazing at the icon of St. Nicholas, and smiling as Bishop Daniel read the prayers for the departure of the soul— are found in "Life and works" [Source 4], "Elder's Diadem" [Source 1], and "The Life of the Venerable Gabriel" [Source 10].

• **Burial without a Coffin:** His specific instruction to be buried without a coffin, wrapped only in his monastic mantle (or a mat/sackcloth), is found in his "Last Will" text [Source 2, 11] and described in the burial accounts in "Life and works" [Source 4] and "Elder's Diadem" [Source 1].

• **The Earth Moving:** The miraculous detail that mourners did not want to throw earth on his body, so they threw it to the side, yet the earth "moved of its own accord" or "flowed down" to cover him respectfully, is recorded in "Life and works" [Source 4] and "The Life of the Venerable Gabriel" [Source 10].

• **"Truth is in the Immortality of the Spirit":** The inscription of these words on his grave, taken from his final teachings, is documented in "Life and works" [Source 4] and "American Carpatho-Russian" [Source 11].

• **Canonization and Relics:** The date of his canonization by the Georgian Synod (December 20, 2012) and the uncovering of his incorrupt relics (February 22, 2014) are found in "OrthoChristian" [Source 2], "The Life of the Venerable Gabriel" [Source 10], and "American Carpatho-Russian" [Source 11].

• **"My Cross is the Whole of Georgia":** His famous statement, "My cross is the whole of Georgia and half of Russia," often cited in the context of his broad veneration, is found in "The Life of the Venerable Gabriel" [Source 10] and "Elder Gabriel Appeared to Me" [Source 12].

- **The Uncovering of the Relics:** The events of February 22, 2014, at Samtavro Convent, where the holy relics were uncovered and found wrapped in a mat (or sackcloth) as he had requested, are documented in "OrthoChristian" [Source 2] and "St. Gabriel Urgebadze" [Source 11]. The immense gathering of the faithful and the translation of the relics to Svetitskhoveli and Sameba Cathedrals are described in "The Life of the Venerable Gabriel" [Source 10] and "OrthoChristian" [Source 2].

- **The Miracle of the Jacket:** The account of pilgrims being allowed to wear Father Gabriel's jacket (which he wore under his mantia) for healing and prayer at the Monastery of the Nativity of the Theotokos is found in "OrthoChristian" [Source 2].

- **Healings of Prisoners:** The specific letters from prisoners attesting to miracles are found in "OrthoChristian" [Source 2]. These include:

  ◦ **Vasiliy Narindoshvili:** Healed of a ruptured eardrum and hearing loss after anointing with oil from the Elder's lampada.

  ◦ **Guram Managadze:** Healed of severe stomach ulcers after drinking the oil.

  ◦ **Artur Soukasyan:** Cured of a rotting/festering foot.

- **Medical Miracles:** Specific accounts of physical healings are sourced from "OrthoChristian" [Source 2], including:

  ◦ **Lela Tsirekidze:** Diagnosed with tumors, she saw a vision of Father Gabriel smiling, refused surgery, and was found cancer-free two months later.

  ◦ **The Child with the Fractured Skull:** A neighbor's child run over by a car, whose swelling went down and who recovered after anointing.

• **Prophecies of the End Times:** Father Gabriel's specific teachings regarding the Antichrist and the Last Days are found in "Elder's Diadem" [Source 1] and "Life and works" [Source 4].

  ◦ **"Antichrist is at the door":** The warning that the Antichrist is not knocking but breaking in, and that people will witness his reign, is from "Elder's Diadem" [Source 1] and "Life and works" [Source 4].

  ◦ **Fleeing to the Mountains:** His instruction to flee to the mountains during the persecution, and the promise that God will provide food (even turning leaves or earth into bread), is found in "Life and works" [Source 4] and "Elder's Diadem" [Source 1].

  ◦ **The "666" Traps:** His warning about the number of the beast and the 666 traps set by Satan is from "Elder's Diadem" [Source 1].

  ◦ **The Iveron Icon:** The prophecy that the Iveron Icon will leave Mount Athos, followed by the tolling of bells, is recorded in "Elder's Diadem" [Source 1] and "Life and works" [Source 4].

• **"My Cross is Georgia":** His statement, "My cross is the whole of Georgia and half of Russia," reflecting the scope of his intercession, is found in "Elder Gabriel Appeared to Me" [Source 12] and "The Life of the Venerable Gabriel" [Source 10].

• **"I Wait for You at Samtavro":** The sentiment that he awaits pilgrims at Samtavro and that those who visit him are "kindred souls" brought together by him is described in "Getting to know Elder Gabriel" [Source 12] and "OrthoChristian" [Source 2].